4 June 93 Fri
$36 + Tax
Tower NYC
(G.I. Path course
Cornell U.)
read ½ at bar
+ on L.I.R.R. to
home.   JM

William Kapell

WILLIAM KAPELL

A Documentary Life History of the American Pianist

Tim Page

International Piano Archives
at the University of Maryland
College Park

Library of Congress Cataloging-in-Publication Data

William Kapell : a documentary life history of the
American pianist / [compiled by] Tim Page.
    p.   cm.
  "The vast majority of the material is drawn
from the Kapell collection at the International
Piano Archives at Maryland"—Introd.
  Discography: p.
  Includes index.
  ISBN 0-89579-298-2 (cloth). —
  ISBN 0-89579-273-7 (pbk.)
  1. Kapell, William, 1922-1953. 2. Pianists—
United States—Biography. I. Kapell, William,
1922-1953. II. Page, Tim, 1954- . III.
International Piano Archives at Maryland.
ML417.K27W5   1992
786.2´092—dc20
    [B]   92-17288
                                           CIP
                                           MN

© Copyright 1992 University of Maryland
at College Park

*For Anna Lou
with love and admiration*

*and for the children and grandchildren
of William Kapell*

Kapell was a pathfinder of the most extraordinarily potent kind. There's a beauty, an aesthetic completeness, about that driven, violent personality, cutting a path through the world, becoming the adored hero of the public, playing ever more beautifully, and finally colliding with a mountain. That's the stuff of legend.

Jerome Lowenthal

Contents

List of Photographers xi

Youth 1

Fame 26

Mastery 110

Afterwards 162

Discography 188

Index 197

List of Photographers

James Abresch, 39

Acme Photo, 66–67, 72–73, 84–85, 91

Associated Newspapers, Ltd., 159

"Bill" Benswanger, 42

Jon Brenneis, 121, 124–25, 122

Byron-Haral Photography, 108

John G. Cole, 186

Sarah de Havenon, 13, 130

El Al, Israel Airlines, Ltd., 150

Florida Photo, 151

Fotos Lydia, 88–89, 109

Larry Gordon, 82–83, 101

Ben Greenhaus, 34, 63, 94, 95

Hope Associates Corp., 41, 99

International Piano Archives at Maryland, 136–37, 186

William Jacobellis, 130

André Kertész, 76–77

Sedge LeBlanq, 131

Logan-Markham, 96

Paul Lubell, 2

Ruth Orkin, 78–79, 80–81

Irving Penn, 186–87, 188

Polkinghorne and Stevens, 159

S. H. Roberts, 67

Noël Ruby photography, Ltd., 16

Athol Shmith, 37, 55

John Stewart, 110

Shapiro Studio, 38, 62–63

Theatrical Studio, 48

Chas. Warner, 65

William Kapell

Introduction

This is not a biography. It is, instead, a collection of documents assembled in honor of an outstanding American musician that will, one hopes, serve not only as a tribute to William Kapell but also as a privileged glimpse into the life of a performing artist during the 1940s and 1950s.

The vast majority of the material is drawn from the Kapell collection at the International Piano Archives at Maryland, a gift of the pianist's widow, Anna Lou Dehavenon. I am grateful to the staff, past and present, of IPAM — especially Neil Ratliff, Morgan Cundiff and Bruce D. Wilson — without whose active support and assistance this book would have been an impossibility.

In addition to the many hours I spent with Dr. Dehavenon, Laura Fratti, Eugene Istomin, Bernard Kapell, Jack Pfeiffer and Solveig Lunde Madsen graciously consented to share reminiscences with me; moreover, with his permission, I have made use of a lively interview Dr. Wilson conducted with Jerome Lowenthal. I owe debts of gratitude to Allan Evans for his authoritative discography; to Cynthia Horton, who brought this project to A-R Editions, and to Patrick Warczak, James Gehrke and everyone at A-R Editions for their beautiful realization of this book; and to my friend from Tanglewood days, Robert Tumarkin, who, one night long ago, introduced a room full of music students to the playing of William Kapell.

Thanks to the staff of WNYC-FM in New York, where my first interview with Dr. Dehavenon was broadcast in 1984; also to Suzanne C. Taylor and Peter Del Toro, who presented a valuable Kapell festival on WKCR-FM in 1987. My editors at *Newsday* were more than accommodating in allowing me the time to finish this project and my family — my wife Vanessa Weeks Page and my children William Dean and Robert Leonard Page — was wonderfully understanding about my long hibernations in the study.

Kapell's real legacy is his recordings; a complete edition is long overdue and would, I think, prove not only inspirational but revelatory to a new generation of pianists.

> Tim Page
> New York City
> March 3, 1992

Part One : Youth

William Kapell was born in New York on September 20, 1922. He was the son of Hyman Kapell (known as Harry) and Edith Wolfson (born Mouletski) Kapell, first generation Polish/Russian emigres who owned and operated a bookstore at 1144 Lexington Avenue on the Upper East Side of Manhattan.

The child's response to music was apparent from an early age. The family owned a Victrola, and Edith Kapell discovered that she could soothe the infant William with certain Mozart recordings. After he began to walk, he took pleasure in reaching up to the keyboard of any piano he saw and hitting the keys with his fingers.

"My parents thought it was important for their children to receive music lessons," Bernard, Kapell's younger brother, recalled in 1992. "Willy took piano lessons from about the age of seven or eight, but my parents stopped them because they said they couldn't afford to pay for them for a child who would not practice. But then, when Willy was about ten, he asked to start lessons again. Now, this would have been 1932 — the depths of the Depression — and my parents simply couldn't afford music lessons. But he was intent, and so they started looking around for a teacher who would work with him for free or at greatly reduced rates."

They found Mrs. Dorothy Anderson LaFollette at the Yorkville Settlement Music School on First Avenue, not far from their home. "She almost immediately saw Willy's genius and started teaching him three days a week at her home," Bernard Kapell remembers. "From then on, he learned very quickly."

Indeed, six weeks after he began with LaFollette, he was selected (along with several other students in settlement schools) to play in the pianist Jose Iturbi's apartment and share a Thanksgiving turkey dinner with him. Edith Kapell had planned to attend but could not escape from bookshop duties that day until the concert had ended. "When she arrived, all the other mothers practically wept at her feet," his brother said. "They told her that she had an extraordinary child — that he was the best by far of the young pianists, and that's not an easy thing for the mother of another pianist to admit!"

Kapell himself would later reflect on his years with LaFollette: "[She] was an angel with me. Sometimes the lessons took three or four hours. I actually did my routine practicing while I was at her house. She took infinite pains. I wonder now and then how she managed never to lose her temper." Anna Lou Dehavenon, who married Kapell in 1948, credits LaFollette with providing the foundation of his technical mastery, while Kapell himself expressed gratitude to her for developing what he called his "rubber wrists."

In the summer of 1935, LaFollette invited Kapell to La Jolla, California, where she was visiting her mother. After a grueling bus trip from New York — these were the days before interstate highways — Kapell had six sunny weeks in which to study and practice. While in La Jolla, he played his first recital, in a beachfront hotel called the Casa de Mañana (it still stands, but has now been converted into a retirement home).

Back in New York, the Kapells, anxious that their son should have enough time to practice, arranged for him to attend Columbia Grammar School on a scholarship. He was by now an indefatigable practicer: according to Bernard Kapell, the family moved every two years (addresses included 315 East 80th Street and 239 East 79th Street) simply because no landlord would renew their lease — "Willy was just too loud," he recalled with a chuckle.

LaFollette encouraged Kapell to play for her teachers, Josef and Rosina Lhevinne, and also for Arthur Rubinstein. According to Rubinstein's second (and not entirely reliable) memoir, *My Many Years*, "Willy Kapell right away became overfriendly with me and tried to amuse me by speaking badly of his teacher, who happened to be my friend Josef Lhevinne. When I reprimanded him, he burst out: 'He doesn't understand me. I have no communication with him. But if you could take me on, I feel I could make real progress.' I refused, point blank. 'You need discipline, young man, and also to be heard often. I am not the right teacher for you because I give too many concerts but I shall always be willing to hear you play whenever possible.'"

Although Kapell and Rubinstein remained in contact for many years, the association was often strained; Kapell considered Rubinstein an extraordinarily gifted musician but more than a little lazy, while Rubinstein was angered by secondhand (but not implausible) reports that Kapell had criticized him. [Readers with an interest in the relationship are referred to Jerome Lowenthal's excellent article, "Memories of William Kapell" in the February 1984 issue of *Clavier*.]

When he was 16, Kapell began studying with Olga Samaroff, initially at the Philadelphia Conservatory and then later at the Juilliard School. A distinguished pianist in her own right (she made many recordings for what was then the Victor Talking Machine Company in the early years of the 20th century) "Madam," as her students inevitably called her, proved the most important direct musical influence on Kapell after LaFollette. (There is some difference of opinion about LaFollette's response to Kapell's decision to study with a more famous and "well-connected" pedagogue. Bernard Kapell recalls a period of estrangement, but Anna Lou Dehavenon believes that LaFollette encouraged the switch, feeling that she had taught him all she could.)

It was around this time that Kapell and his brother were caught sneaking into a concert at Carnegie Hall. "It used to be easy to do," according to Bernard Kapell, "but this time an usher found us just as we were coming down the stairs, and he threw us out. And I remember Willy got very angry and told the usher that he was going to be up on that stage playing some day. And, of course, he was, and not very long after."

In 1940, Kapell entered Juilliard, where he continued his studies with Samaroff. There he met Solveig Lunde (known as "Dorothy" or "Dophey"), another Samaroff student, who became his first serious girlfriend. The relationship was, by all accounts, a stormy one — Kapell's intensity was not confined to his pianism — but it would continue, in one form or another, for some seven years.

During his freshman semester at Juilliard, Kapell won the 1940 Youth Contest of the Philadelphia Orchestra and made his debut with the ensemble, under its music director, Eugene Ormandy, at the Academy of Music on February 10, 1941. He made a great success and was invited back to Philadelphia that summer to play in the Robin Hood Dell series under the direction of Charles O'Connell. (O'Connell was also the artistic director of RCA Victor, which became Kapell's record company; this was the first time he heard him play.)

In the fall of 1941, Kapell was ready to take on New York. As winner of the Walter W. Naumburg Musical Foundation Award, he was entitled to a debut at Town Hall, which he played on October 28. The program consisted of works by Bach, Chopin, Brahms, Albeniz, Medtner, Rachmaninoff and Shostakovich.

It was a brave and unusual program for a 19-year old boy to undertake. Kapell offered selections from the "Well Tempered Clavier" and the Suite in A Minor at a time when Bach's music was presented in piano concerts less often than it is today. (Glenn Gould, who did so much to change the repertory, played his New York debut on the same stage 14 years later.) The largest work on the program was the Brahms Sonata in C (Op. 1), which contains some wonderful music but is not particularly flattering to a pianist and is consequently rarely heard to this day. Moreover, even at the beginning of his career, Kapell demonstrated a clear interest in the music of his own time; three of the seven composers on the program — Medtner, Rachmaninoff and Shostakovich — were still active.

The concert was a popular and critical success. Howard Taubman, a young reviewer for the *New York Times* who would later succeed Olin Downes as the chief critic for that newspaper from 1955 to 1960, called Kapell "a generously gifted pianist, one of the most talented to appear under the beneficent wing of the Naumburg Foundation." "He has more than enough technique, but, more important, he has imagination and sensitivity," Taubman added.

Jerome D. Bohm, writing in the New York *Herald Tribune*, was even more enthusiastic: "Mr. Kapell's work left me with a feeling of exhilaration not often carried away from the concert hall . . . . His enkindling imagination and sensitivity found their fullest expression in the F major ballade of Chopin which was not brilliantly performed from the technical aspect but with something rarely encountered these days, a true flair for the Polish Master's idiom, with its blend of morbidezza and passion. I shall consider myself fortunate if I hear another performance of the F major ballade this season as satisfying as this one."

The word went out within New York's tightly-knit musical establishment: William Kapell, not yet out of his teens, was already an exciting pianist.

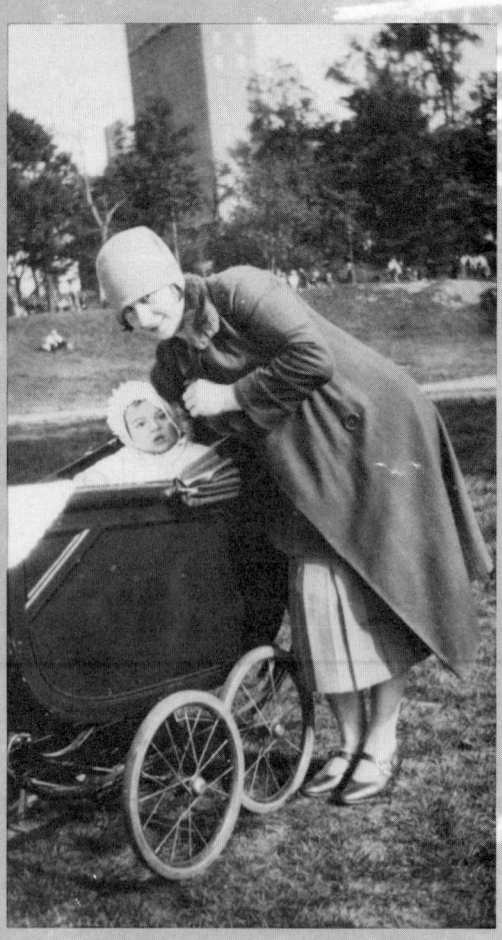

Kapell as an infant, out for a stroller ride with his mother, Edith. The setting is likely Central Park, a few blocks from the Upper East Side neighborhood where Kapell grew up and lived most of his life.

It is always dangerous to read too much into photographs, but one has the clear sense of a proud, determined and, perhaps, rather imperious toddler from these two early snapshots of Kapell as a young child (left and background).

Kapell on a Brooklyn beach with his father Harry, about 1926. "We knew next to nothing about my father's background," Bernard Kapell said in 1992. "Whenever we'd ask him about his early life, he'd become very mysterious and change the subject." (Above) A period piece from the 1920s: young Kapell in an outgrown suit, antique car in the background.

Although the Kapell family was not especially well off, Edith Kapell made sure that the family escaped the heat and grime of Manhattan summers in a succession of rented houses on Long Island. All of the photographs on these two pages were taken during such vacations. The boy with Kapell below is his brother Bernard, born in 1926.

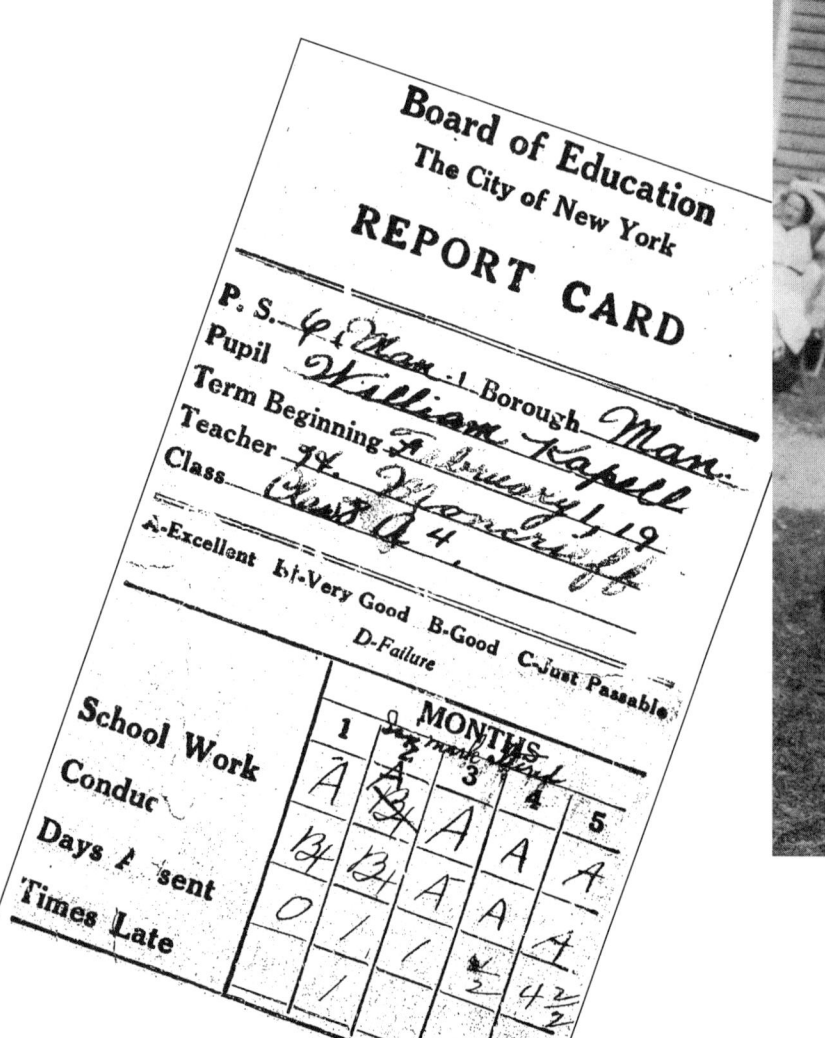

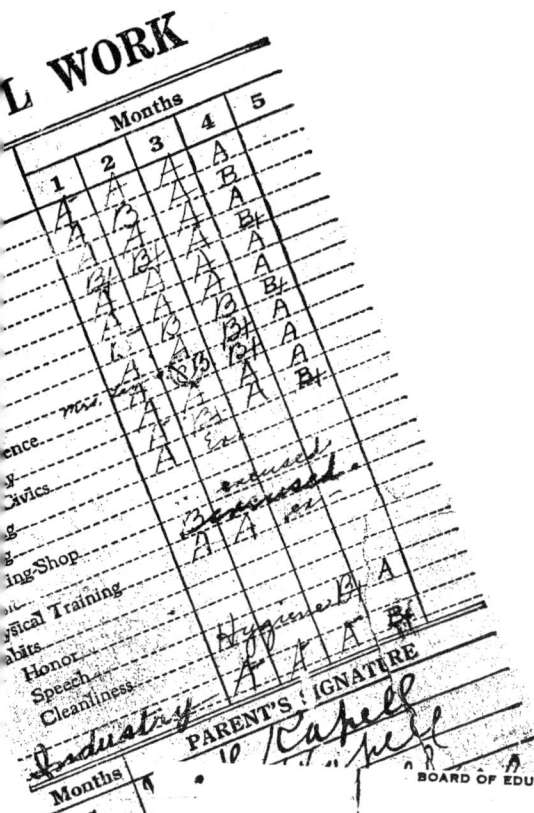

BOARD OF EDUCATION OF THE CITY OF NEW YORK

PUBLIC SCHOOL NO. 6
39 EAST 85TH STREET
NEW YORK, N.Y.

November 26th, 1935

To Whom it May Concern:

The bearer, Mrs. Hyman Kappel, is the mother of William Kappel, a student in this school, who will be ready to enter high school on February 1st, 1935. The boy is unusually gifted musically. He is planning a professional career for himself and is anxious to have his high school work contribute as much as possible toward that end.

The difficulty of securing in a public high school the kind of program that William will require for the next four years has forced the boy's parents to look about for other possibilities. It was suggested to them by friends that your school might consider taking him on a scholarship. Mrs. Kappel's purpose in presenting herself therefore, is to talk the matter over with the person in charge of scholarships.

William's school record is exceptionally good. He is a boy of high intelligence, splendid character and good instincts. His work has always been superior. His ability as a pianist is of such a high order that in the future it will be a credit to any institution to have had a part in furthering his ambitions.

Very truly yours,

Emily Nosworthy

EMILY NOSWORTHY
Principal

Kapell was a diligent student, well-liked by his teachers. A disproportionate number of valuable musicians have attended the New York public schools. Still, the Kapells were concerned that their son have enough time to practice and, to that end, they sought his enrollment in private school. To the left is the letter from the Principal of P.S. 6, Emily Nosworthy, that Edith Kapell presented in several interviews before Kapell was accepted as a scholarship student at Columbia Grammar School. (Note the misspelling of his name, which would plague the pianist for much of his career.)

11

Kapell with Dorothy LaFollette, his first important teacher, in La Jolla, California. From the beginning, LaFollette was convinced the boy was a genius, and she devoted several days a week to his tutelage. Kapell and his mother made the grueling, cross-country bus trip to California so that he could spend an entire summer studying with LaFollette.

La Jolla was then a village of some 3000 people — a radical change from congested Manhattan. Kapell took to Southern California immediately and spent a considerable amount of time there over the course of his life.

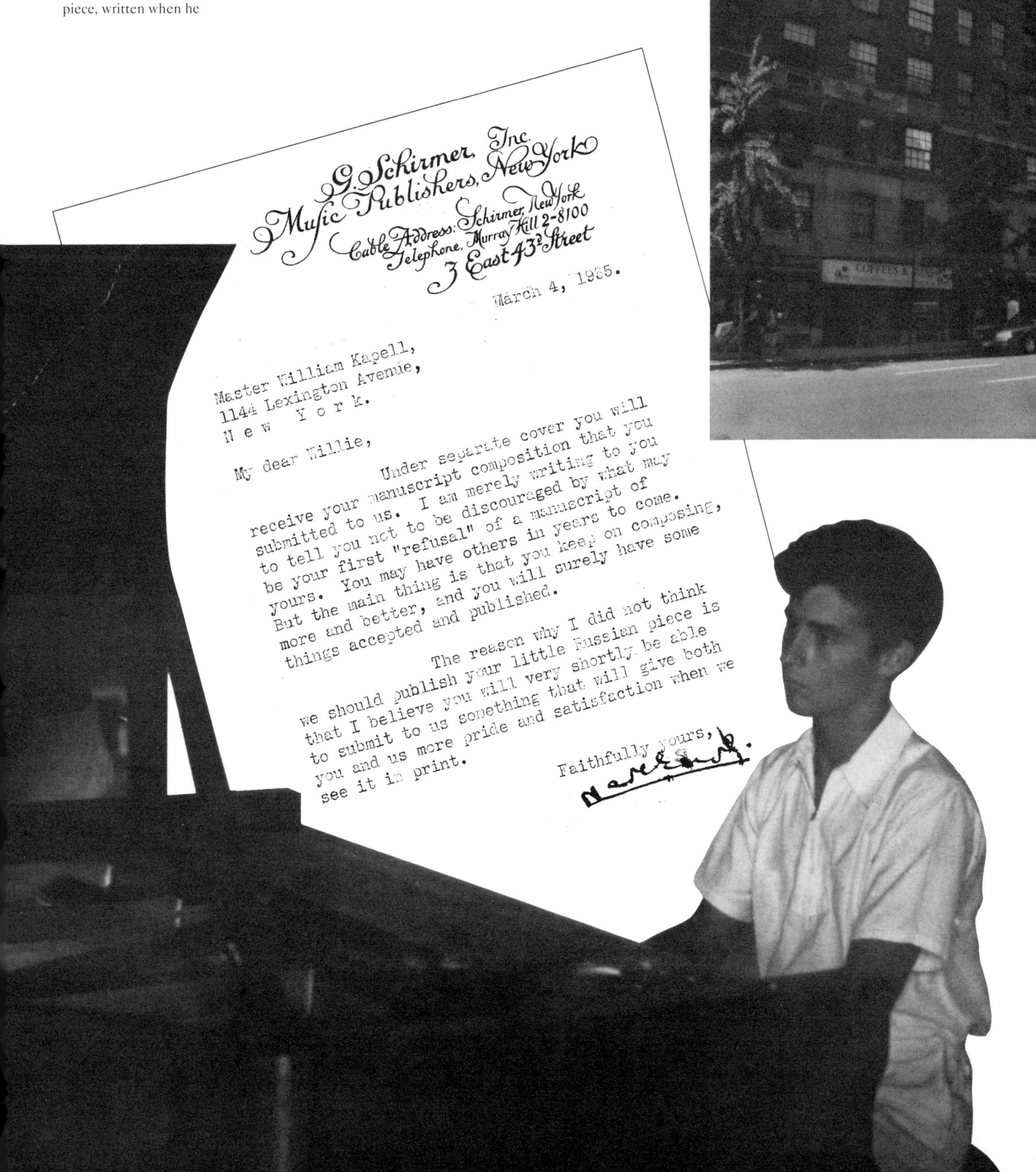

Kapell at the piano, lost in reverie. The photograph probably dates from the mid-30s. (Below) From an early age, Kapell was fascinated by all aspects of music, including composition. One piece, written when he was barely in his teens, inspired this remarkably thoughtful and encouraging rejection letter from one of the country's leading music publishers. (Right) Harry and Edith Kapell ran a bookstore on the ground level of 1144 Lexington Avenue, seen here in a 1992 photograph.

> G. Schirmer, Inc.
> Music Publishers, New York
> Cable Address: Schirmer, New York
> Telephone, Murray Hill 2-8100
> 3 East 43d Street
>
> March 4, 1935.
>
> Master William Kapell,
> 1144 Lexington Avenue,
> New York.
>
> My dear Willie,
>
> Under separate cover you will receive your manuscript composition that you submitted to us. I am merely writing to you to tell you not to be discouraged by what may be your first "refusal" of a manuscript of yours. You may have others in years to come. But the main thing is that you keep on composing, more and better, and you will surely have some things accepted and published.
>
> The reason why I did not think we should publish your little Russian piece is that I believe you will very shortly be able to submit to us something that will give both you and us more pride and satisfaction when we see it in print.
>
> Faithfully yours,

In 1938, Kapell began his studies with Olga Samaroff, whom he called "Madam," and worked with her at the Philadelphia Conservatory and at Juilliard. It is Samaroff's handwriting at the top of Kapell's copy of the Chopin Nocturne in B-flat Minor (Op. 9, No. 1). These photographs, taken some time later show (upper left) Kapell and Eugene List flanking Samaroff and (lower left) "Madam" with a gathering of her students; Eugene List and Kapell, Solveig Lunde, known as "Dophey," sits immediately to Samaroff's left. (Right) Like many adolescents, Kapell suffered from complexion problems. He looks awkward and uncomfortable in this performance photograph taken in the late 30s.

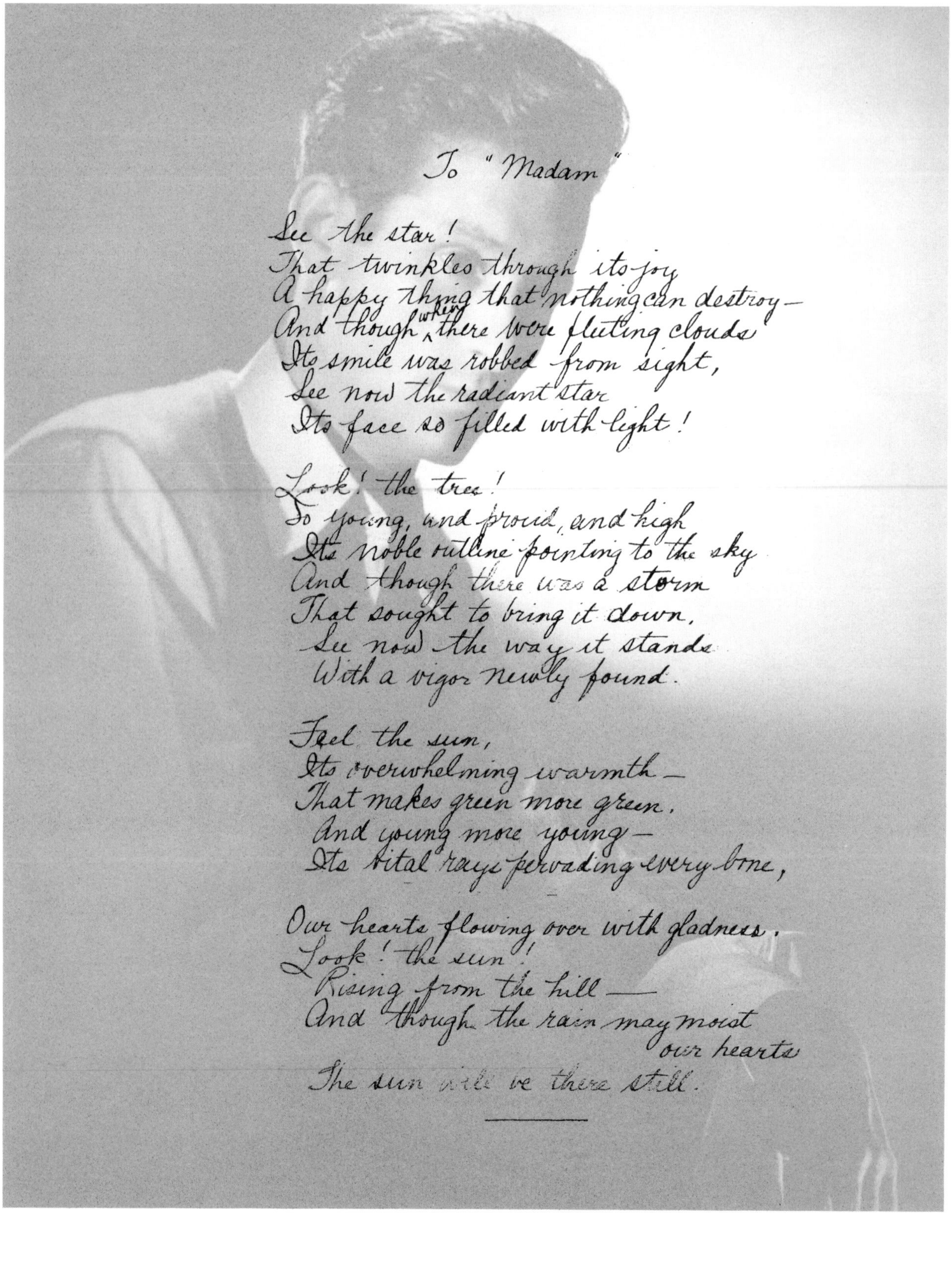

To "Madam"

See the star!
That twinkles through its joy
A happy thing that nothing can destroy—
And though when there were fleeting clouds
Its smile was robbed from sight,
See now the radiant star
Its face so filled with light!

Look! the tree!
So young, and proud, and high
Its noble outline pointing to the sky.
And though there was a storm
That sought to bring it down,
See now the way it stands
With a vigor newly found.

Feel the sun,
Its overwhelming warmth—
That makes green more green.
And young more young—
Its vital rays pervading every bone,

Our hearts flowing over with gladness.
Look! the sun!
Rising from the hill——
And though the rain may moist
                    our hearts
The sun will be there still.

———

To Willy
with infinite pride
and joy I'm that growth
of his art and also in the development
of "the man behind his art."
affectionately
"Madam"

May. 1942.

Herbert Mitchell

One of Kapell's compositions, probably dating from the late 30s. He also tried his hand at popular songs.

The Naumburg family and its foundation have supported many young artists over the years. The Walter W. Naumburg Award allowed the 19-year-old Kapell to play his first solo recital in October, 1941. The venue was Town Hall, at 123 West 43rd Street in midtown Manhattan; it is still in use today.

Dear Mr. Naumburg,

I am afraid that words are futile as a means of expressing the deep gratitude I feel, but I hope that they convey a little of it to you.

Thank you for making it possible, through the kindness of your heart, for young musicians to have a way to give their first big concert. I feel that I am very lucky indeed, to have been given this wonderful opportunity. I will try to live up to it.

I wish I could tell you what my heart feels, but the more I write, the more impossible it becomes. I can only say,

Thank you from the bottom of my heart, William Kapell

Kapell had been playing at informal musicales around New York for some time (previous page), but his recital at Town Hall established him as an important young pianist in the city of his birth.

THE TOWN HALL

123 WEST 43rd STREET, NEW YORK, N. Y.

William Kapell

fred Scott • Publisher • 156 Fifth Avenue, New York

Town Hall Program

THE TOWN HALL
SEASON 1941-1942

FIRE NOTICE:—Look around NOW and choose the nearest Exit to your seat. In case of fire walk (not run) to THAT Exit. Do not try to beat your neighbor to the street.
PATRICK J. WALSH, *Fire Commissioner*

Tuesday Afternoon, October 28, at 2:45 o'clock

WILLIAM KAPELL
American Pianist

Winner of the Walter W. Naumburg Foundation Award

Program

I.

Prelude and Fugue, C sharp minor (Book I) .... Bach
Suite A minor (from miscellaneous works) .... Bach
    Allemande
        Courante
            Sarabande, simple
                Sarabande, double
                    Gigue

II.

Sonata, C major, Op. 1 .... Brahms
    Allegro
        Andante (Nach einem altdeutschen Minneliede)
        Scherzo, allegro molto e con fuoco
        Finale, allegro con fuoco

— *Intermission* —

Program Continued on Second Page Following

NEW *Recording Studio*
ON THE FIFTH FLOOR
SCHIRMER BUILDING
Two large studios, with most modern equipment, acoustically treated by experts. Excellent grand pianos. Vocal and instrumental recordings.
Studio Recordings as low as $1.00

GSCHIRMER   3 E. 43rd ST., NEW YORK
Telephone: MUrray Hill 2-8100

WEDNESDAY, OCTOBER 2

CONTEST WINNER HEARD IN RECITAL

William Kapell, Pianist, Plays at Town Hall

By OSCAR THOMPSON

Of recent Naumburg winners, none has made a more favorable first impression than William Kapell, 19-year-old pianist, left with the audience that heard him in Town Hall yesterday afternoon. His was playing of technical brilliance and no small measure of imagination. His tone was of a singing quality and there was warmth of feeling as well as security and style in his performances. All in all, he made an uncommon showing.

Like many another, young Mr. Kapell began his program with Bach—the Prelude and Fugue in C sharp minor from Book I of the "Well-Tempered Clavichord." More Bach followed, the Suite in A minor. If the latter smacked of routine, it was clearly, and vigorously delineated. The ornaments of the Prelude were finely set forth. The Fugue was given more than a touch of individuality and was essentially alive.

To the Brahms Sonata in C major, No. 1, the recitalist brought a boldness and a surety that ordinarily are to be expected of the experienced virtuoso. The rhythmic power of the opening passage was made felt and the finale variation of the andante was exquisitely set forth. In the scherzo and the finale there was a tendency to excessive speed and some clipping of chords.

Notable in a Chopin group was an altogether persuasive achievement of the F major Ballade. Also on the program were Rachmaninoff's Prelude in E flat major; Medtner's "Fairy Tale" in B flat minor, three Shostakovitch preludes, and Albeniz's "Evocation" and "Triana." The applause was of a heartiness to indicate more than everyday enthusiasm.

HERALD TRIBUNE

Kapell, 19, Gives Piano Recital, Prize for Work

Winner of Naumburg Foundation Award Plays Difficult Program at Town Hall

By Jerome D. Bohm

On the strength of the accomplishments revealed at his recital, which constituted the award of the Walter N. Naumburg Foundation in Town Hall yesterday afternoon, William Kapell, nineteen-year-old American pianist, must be considered among the most worth while of our younger players. In a program which held the Prelude and Fugue in C sharp minor from the first book of Bach's "Well-Tempered Clavichord," and Suite in A minor, Brahms's Sonata in C major, Op. 1, a Chopin group comprising the Ballade in F major, Nocturne in B major, Op. 62, No. 1, two mazurkas and the Barcarolle, and compositions by Rachmaninoff, Medtner, Shostakovitch and Albeniz, Mr. Kapell's work left me with a feeling of exhilaration not often carried away from the concert hall.

Mr. Kapell has mastered the externals of his art to an exceptional degree. His technical equipment is that of a true virtuoso. The most taxing pages in the Brahms sonata were traversed with deceptive ease, although it must be admitted that the passages in thirds in the finale were played too fast to permit them to emerge as clearly as one would have liked them to. But this was one of the few instances in which Mr. Kapell's poise was not complete, or of the few in which his youthful ardor led to an excess of speed. Otherwise his interpretation of this early product of Brahms was genuinely impressive. Although slightly bulky Mr. Kapell, because he has mastered the problem of muscular relaxation, knows how to obtain a fortissimo which is sonorous without being brittle. His conception revealed much of the music's passionate sweep in the sonata's three quick movements, and the restrained yet indubitable sensibility disclosed in the andante spoke well for the player's taste and sense of style.

Mr. Kapell's treatment of the Bach prelude and fugue was completely sound and his healthy musical approach and rhythmic security were equally apparent in the A minor suite. His enkindling imagination and sensitivity found their fullest expression in the major ballade of Chopin, which was not brilliantly performed from the technical aspect, but with something rarely encountered these days, a true flair for the Polish master's idiom, with its blend of morbidezza and passion. I shall consider myself fortunate if I hear another performance of the F major ballade this season as satisfying as this one was.

A sampling of the press response to Kapell's Town Hall debut: Oscar Thompson in the New York *Sun*, Jerome D. Bohm in the New York *Herald Tribune* and Howard Taubman in the *New York Times*. (It was then *Times* practice to run reviews by junior critics signed only with initials.)

William Kapell's Debut

William Kapell, 18-year-old New Yorker, has often dropped into Town Hall, as local music students do, to hear musicians in their debuts. Yesterday afternoon he was at the Town Hall again, but this time he was making his debut as a pianist, and a host of students were there to watch and hear, suffer and triumph with him. As a winner of a Walter W. Naumburg Foundation award, young Mr. Kapell was collecting his prize, a New York debut.

If the young pianist has thought in recent years that he could do as well as or better than many of the newcomers, he had good reason. He is a generously gifted pianist, one of the most talented to appear under the beneficent wing of the Naumburg Foundation. He has more than enough technique, but, more important, he has imagination and sensitivity. His playing of the Chopin F major Ballade had breadth of design and maturity of feeling. His Bach was clean cut; his Brahms—the Sonata in C, Op. 1—was properly ardent. There were other works by Chopin and by Rachmaninoff, Medtner, Shostakovich and Albeniz.

Mr. Kapell has considerable balance for a pianist in his teens, but it would be unnatural if he did not have some of the qualities of youth. He took some tempi at a breakneck speed, but he did not come to grief as far as the notes were concerned; the Brahms sonata, treated in this fashion in some places, however, did seem a bit breathless and piqued. The young pianist strove generally for a singing tone, but occasionally his desire for a big voice betrayed him into harshness. These are minor things compared with the young man's insight as a musician and his flair for the piano. He should be spending a good deal of his time on the performing side of the footlights in seasons to come.

H. T.

Part Two : Fame

*A*rthur Judson was probably the closest thing to a musical czar the United States ever had. At the height of his career, he managed not only two of our leading orchestras — the New York Philharmonic and the Philadelphia Orchestra — but most of the important conductors in the industry, as well as many soloists. Under his direction, Columbia Concerts (later Columbia Artists) became far and away the most powerful musical management company in the world, a position it enjoys to this day.

And, in February, 1942, under Samaroff's watchful eye, Judson himself signed William Kapell to a three-year contract. Over the next eleven years, Kapell would tour the country and the world, in community concerts and as a "headliner." He played regularly, not only in recital, but with most of the major American orchestras; he was a favorite partner of such conductors as Eugene Ormandy, Leopold Stokowski, Fritz Reiner and Leonard Bernstein.

It was, by turn, both a glamorous life and a deeply draining one. If celebrity as a performing musician meant service to a beloved art, applause and glittering dinners, it also meant submitting to inane publicity, making awkward train connections in the middle of the night, and playing on less-than-adequate pianos in dreary small towns. Kapell's later diaries — in which he kept careful track of the audiences, critics and instruments (unless he had taken his own piano) in the places he visited — are remarkably immediate documents. His dedication is clear, his triumphs are vividly set down, but the overriding sense that a reader is left with is isolation and loneliness. Indeed, most of the happiest passages in the journals are those penned at home in New York — and in his beloved California.

In July 1942, conductor Efrem Kurtz personally selected Kapell to play Aram Khachaturian's Piano Concerto with the New York Philharmonic at Manhattan's old Lewisohn Stadium. Thereafter, he played it dozens of times with various orchestras throughout this country and abroad (including one memorable performance before a Philadelphia audience that included the young Andrei Gromyko). It was, without a doubt (and to the pianist's later chagrin) William Kapell's "greatest hit."

The concerto became popular in the early years of World War II, during the United States/Soviet Union United Front against fascism, at a time when relationships between the two new superpowers were at an all-time high and there was a great Western vogue for things Russian. This may help explain the meteoric (although rather brief) enthusiasm for this concerto — this, and Kapell's vibrant, energetic espousal of Khachaturian's sturdy tunes.

An unusual symbiosis developed between Kapell and the Khachaturian concerto; if the pianist's many performances of this work helped establish his career, it may also be said that Kapell virtually made the concerto. Although he did not (as has been reported) play the American premiere, he did make the first recording — with Serge Koussevitzky and the Boston Symphony Orchestra — and ever since it was released on 78s in 1946, the Kapell performance has been the standard by which all others must be judged.

However, Kapell had made a more important recording the previous year. This was a staggeringly virtuosic, breathtakingly theatrical and prismatically colored performance of Liszt's "Mephisto Waltz No. 1" (usually called, simply, the "Mephisto Waltz," although the composer wrote three more) — nine minutes and forty-five seconds of furious energy that still, almost half a century later, retains the power to amaze.

Vladimir Horowitz was Kapell's pianistic hero at this stage in his career and the early recordings are in the forceful, muscular, aggressively brilliant, goal-oriented — and often very exciting — Horowitz manner. The later discs are more spacious and serene (although what impresses us in a live recording of the Chopin B-flat Minor Sonata made at his last concert is, above all else, its tragic, personal sense of urgency). After 1947, Kapell came under the influence of some very different musicians — among them his friend Eugene Istomin, Pablo Casals, Rudolf Serkin and Artur Schnabel (according to Leon Fleisher, Schnabel once tuned in to a New York radio station and mistook Kapell's recording of Beethoven's second piano concerto for one of his own). Kapell later studied with Schnabel and yoked a new ease and gentle lyricism to his phenomenal energy and "daemonic" power.

That power and energy, attested to by virtually everybody who heard Kapell play and borne out in the recordings, was not easily won. Kapell was a tremendously hard worker. "Even on the days when he was traveling from one city to the next, he would organize the travel schedule and make appointments ahead of time to be able to practice in the evening at the local Steinway store," Anna Lou Dehavenon recalled in 1984. "And the diaries show that he worked pretty consistently an average of four or five hours every day — sometimes less and sometimes more."

Kapell had other interests besides music. He was a voracious reader, loved a good movie, and became a competent painter. He was proud of a small Picasso painting he picked up in France; his long-time patron Fredric Mann advanced him the $1500 he required to make the purchase. He took an active interest in politics and was a particular admirer of Adlai Stevenson. According to Bernard Kapell, he was "a liberal democrat and very pro-Jewish — not really religious but very proud of his heritage and excited about the creation of Israel."

But music was unquestionably the principal force in Kapell's life. "He could not be in a home with a piano for very long without finding his way to the keyboard," Dehavenon said in 1991, "and if there was no piano in the house, he was distinctly uncomfortable. He was insatiably curious about music. Wherever he went, he wanted to know who the pianists and teachers were in each city. I remember early in 1948, after a community concert in Freeport, Illinois, he discovered that there was an elderly lady — oh, she must have been in her late 70s or early 80s — at the reception who had studied with some legendary pianist in France many years before . . . Isidor Philipp, I think. And Willy sat her down right then and there and took a lesson from her. She was delighted, of course."

Kapell's playing was generally rated highly by critics, and two of the most influential music writers in the business — Claudia Cassidy of the Chicago *Tribune* and Virgil Thomson of the New York *Herald Tribune* — were vociferous admirers. "He not only has brilliance, but subtlety, and a fine wide streak of integrity," Cassidy reported in 1946. "It is hard to find a more revealing combination in music."

Still, Kapell received an occasional unfavorable review. Sometimes, he was able to be sanguine about it, complaining only to his diary. ("Stupid remarks about 'muffing' passage in Mussorgsky. Didn't 'muff' a thing.") Other times, he would brood for days. Noel Straus, a critic for the *New York Times*, wrote several prominent slams. This one, after a Carnegie Hall concert on February 28, 1945, must have stung:

> Considering the success of his earlier appearances in this city, Mr. Kapell's playing yesterday evening was disappointing, whether viewed from the purely pianistic or the interpretive angle. All of his performances were technically glib and fluent. But the tone employed had grown percussive and was invariably brash and metallic in the fortissimi constantly resorted to under the mistaken notion that pounding is synonymous with power. Rhythms were restless and unsteady, while energy and brilliance, rather than imagination, insight and inner life, characterized the series of readings.

After Straus panned another, later Carnegie Hall recital, Samaroff sat down and wrote a letter to the editor of the *Times*. She said that the concert had been recorded and invited the critic to substantiate his remarks: "If Mr. Straus can back up his recent statements with any convincing factual proof that would justify them, I shall gladly sit at his feet and learn what may have escaped me during my ten-year European musical education, my personal association with many of the world's greatest artists and my 20 years experience in teaching which includes the concert preparation of several of the most outstanding and successful young pianists now before the public." Samaroff never mailed the letter, but a copy exists in the International Piano Archives at Maryland.

Of course, much of the press devoted to Kapell was of a frivolous nature. Constance Hope, who was perhaps the leading classical music publicist of her time, was briefly engaged for Kapell in the mid-1940s, and she helped ensure that newspapers in Kalamazoo, Zanesville, Terre Haute and assorted Springfields all ran pictures of the pianist painting in his backyard. Gossip columnists compared him to Sinatra; headlines let the world know that "Kapell Likes His Beef Rare, Music Straight." He posed with dogs, with children — even, on one memorable occasion in Australia, with a kangaroo — most of the time looking excruciatingly uncomfortable. Those purists who believe the commercialization of classical music is a recent phenomenon should take a look through the press scrapbooks of William Kapell — preferably to the accompaniment of Enrico Caruso's recording of "Over There."

Yet, despite the exhausting tours, despite the silly publicity, Kapell was continuing to grow. In addition to showpieces by Prokofiev and Rachmaninoff, he recorded the Brahms F minor Sonata for Piano and Viola with William Primrose and the Beethoven Piano Concerto No. 2 with the NBC Symphony under Vladimir Golschmann. He was fiercely critical of his fellow pianists — "You played like a pig!" he once informed his friend Gary Graffman — but was even more critical of himself. As late as 1952, Kapell, one of the supreme masters of his instrument, entered in his diary: "My facility is 'for the birds!' But I do have patience. If 'practice makes perfect,' I should be perfect. Too bad I'm not. But no one is. I shall patiently work on my fingers until they can do what I want them to do."

On February 27, 1947, Kapell received some criticism from an unexpected source. He had played the Rachmaninoff Piano Concerto No. 2 with the Chicago Symphony in a WGN radio broadcast. After the performance, he was introduced to a young pianist named Rebecca Anna Lou Melson, who was then studying at the University of Chicago and at DePaul University with Sergei Tarnowsky and had come backstage only under protest.

Anna Lou had grown up in Portland, Oregon where she studied first with Jessie Lewis, who had been a student of Rafael Joseffy and a protege of Victor Herbert. She attended Reed College, and worked in Tarnowsky's summer master classes (other Tarnowsky pupils, over the course of his long career, included Horowitz, Alexander Uninsky, and Horacio Gutierrez) before coming to Chicago at his invitation.

"I had been invited to the concert with Mildred Kuyper, the wife of George Kuyper, the manager of the Chicago Symphony," she recalled in 1991. "And I thought he'd played much too fast and I didn't want to tell him that. But Mildred insisted and so I came along. Sure enough, when he found out I was a piano student, he asked me what I thought. And I told him that I thought he'd played magnificently but where was the fire? I told him it was so fast that I couldn't hear what he was doing. I forget what he said after that, but a few moments later, Mildred and George asked him for dinner before the orchestra's concert the next evening. And Willy pointed at me and said, yes, if you bring her."

"The dinner the next night started off as a disaster — it had already been arranged that Willy would sit with another woman friend, and he had asked Mildred if she would have me sit with her during the concert and then join him afterwards. I was furious — but Willy took me downstairs later and played the Rachmaninoff Rhapsody for me. I was flattered by his persistence and just stunned by his playing and we quickly became friends."

Fifteen months later, in a civil ceremony in Chicago on May 18, 1948, William Kapell and Rebecca Anna Lou Melson were married.

An early professional photo, taken around the time of Kapell's Town Hall debut. The pianist and composer Abram Chasins called the young pianist "A powerhouse, but a powerhouse with *poetry*."

Still a teenager and a student at Juilliard, Kapell signs an exclusive three-year contract with Arthur Judson, the founder and president of Columbia Concerts, as Samaroff looks on proudly. (Right) Fredric Mann, a wealthy businessman and patron of the arts who became Kapell's devoted mentor.

Kapell honed his art in recitals throughout the country. This photograph, dating from shortly after the beginning of World War II, was taken at a USO concert in Charleston, South Carolina.

FOURTH SYMPHONY CONCERTS
Saturday Evening, November 27, at 8:30
Sunday Afternoon, November 28, at 3:30

Soviet-American Friendship Concerts

(Program to commemorate the tenth anniversary of diplomatic relations between U. S. A. and U. S. S. R. The actual date of recognition of the Soviet Union by the U. S. A. was Nov. 16, 1933. In view of the mighty struggle now being waged by the Red Army against our common enemy and the need for close collaboration between our country, the Soviet Union and the other United Nations in the postwar world, the Saint Louis Symphony Orchestra thinks it most fitting and is happy to dedicate the program to American-Soviet friendship.)

Soloist — WILLIAM KAPELL — Pianist

"STAR SPANGLED BANNER"
"INTERNATIONALE"

VAN VACTOR — Overture for
(First Saint Louis Performances)

PROKOFIEFF — "Classical" Sym
 ALLEGRO
 LARGHETTO
 GAVOTTA
 FINALE

SHOSTAKOVITCH — Polka and Da
"T

GOULD —
(First Saint Louis Performances)
 PROCLAMATION
 SERMON
 A LITTLE BIT OF SIN
 PROTEST
 JUBILEE

INTERMISSION

KHATCHATURIAN —
(First Saint Louis Performances)
 ALLEGRO MAESTOSO
 ANDANTE
 ALLEGRO BRILLANTE

WILLIAM KAPELL
MR. KAPELL PLAYS THE STEINWA

NEXT WEEK — ALEXANDER KIPNIS, renowned Russian
See Page 98 for complete program.

NOW ON THE AIR—Saint Louis Symphony Orchestra, under direction
every Thursday at 9:15 p.m. on KXOK.

— 83 —

The Khachaturian Piano Concerto, composed in 1936, quickly became Kapell's first "signature" piece after he played it with the New York Philharmonic in 1942. Indeed, so closely associated was he with this work that one critic dubbed him "Khachaturian Kapell."

THE PHILADELPHIA ORCHESTRA
FORTY-FOURTH SEASON, 1943-1944

FOURTEENTH PROGRAM
Friday Afternoon, January 14, at Two-thirty
Saturday Evening, January 15, at Eight-thirty

EUGENE ORMANDY Conducting
WILLIAM KAPELL, Pianist

UNITED NATIONS CYCLE
Fifth program—Honoring The Union of Soviet Socialist Republics

National Anthem of the Soviet Union

The Star-Spangled Banner

KABALEVSKY . . . . . Overture, "Colas Breugnon"
First time at these concerts

SHOSTAKOVICH . . . . "Lady Macbeth of Mtsensk"—
Three Fragments
Transcribed by Quinto Maginini
 I. Allegro—Burying the Corpse in the Cellar
 II. Andante—The Ghost disappears
 III. Allegro non troppo—The Drunks at the Wedding

KHATCHATOURIAN . . . . Piano Concerto
 I. Allegro ma non troppo e maestoso
 II. Andante con anima
 III. Allegro brillante
WILLIAM KAPELL
First time at these concerts

INTERMISSION

*TCHAIKOVSKY . . . Symphony No. 4, in F minor, Op. 36
 I. Andante sostenuto—moderato con anima
 II. Andantino in modo di canzona
 III. Scherzo; pizzicato ostinato
 IV. Finale—allegro con fuoco

The STEINWAY is the official piano of The Philadelphia Orchestra
Columbia Records   * Available on VICTOR Records

A professional photograph of Kapell from the early 40s. This was a favorite picture of the pianist's wife, who thought it represented the "Byronic" side of Kapell.

Immediately after his graduation from the Juilliard School, Kapell spent a summer in the Berkshire mountains, where this photograph was taken.

A community concert Program from Wayne, PA

The Tri-County Concerts Association

"ART IS THE GREAT UNIFYING INFLUENCE WHICH MAKES HARMONIOUS LIFE AMONG MEN POSSIBLE"

SECOND CONCERT, 1943 - 1944 Season
RADNOR HIGH SCHOOL   FRIDAY, NOVEMBER

WILLIAM KAPELL
Pianist

PROGRAM

I.

Le Cou-Cou
Fantasy and Fugue in G minor

II.

Sonata in G minor, Op. 22
   So rasch wie moglich
   Andantino
   Scherzo
   Finale

III.

Etude, G flat major, Op. 10
Nocturne, B major, Op. 62
Polonaise, A flat major, Op. 53

INTERMISSION

IV.

                                          Schubert-Rachmaninoff
The Brooklet   Scriabine
Etude, C-sharp minor, Op. 21, No. 1   Rachmaninoff
Prelude, G minor, Op. 23

V.

Spanish Dance, from "La Vida Breve"   DeFalla
Evocation   Albeniz
Triana   Albeniz

CONCERT MANAGEMENT ARTHUR JUDSON, INC.
Division of Columbia Concerts, Inc.
113 West 57th Street   New York, 19, N. Y.

STEINWAY PIANO

Of all the conductors with whom he worked, Kapell was closest to Eugene Ormandy of the Philadelphia Orchestra. (Below) It was sometimes necessary to make impromptu cuts in compositions in order to accommodate commercial radio broadcasts.

Kapell with Dorothy LaFollette and a new generation of her students, for whom he endowed a scholarship.

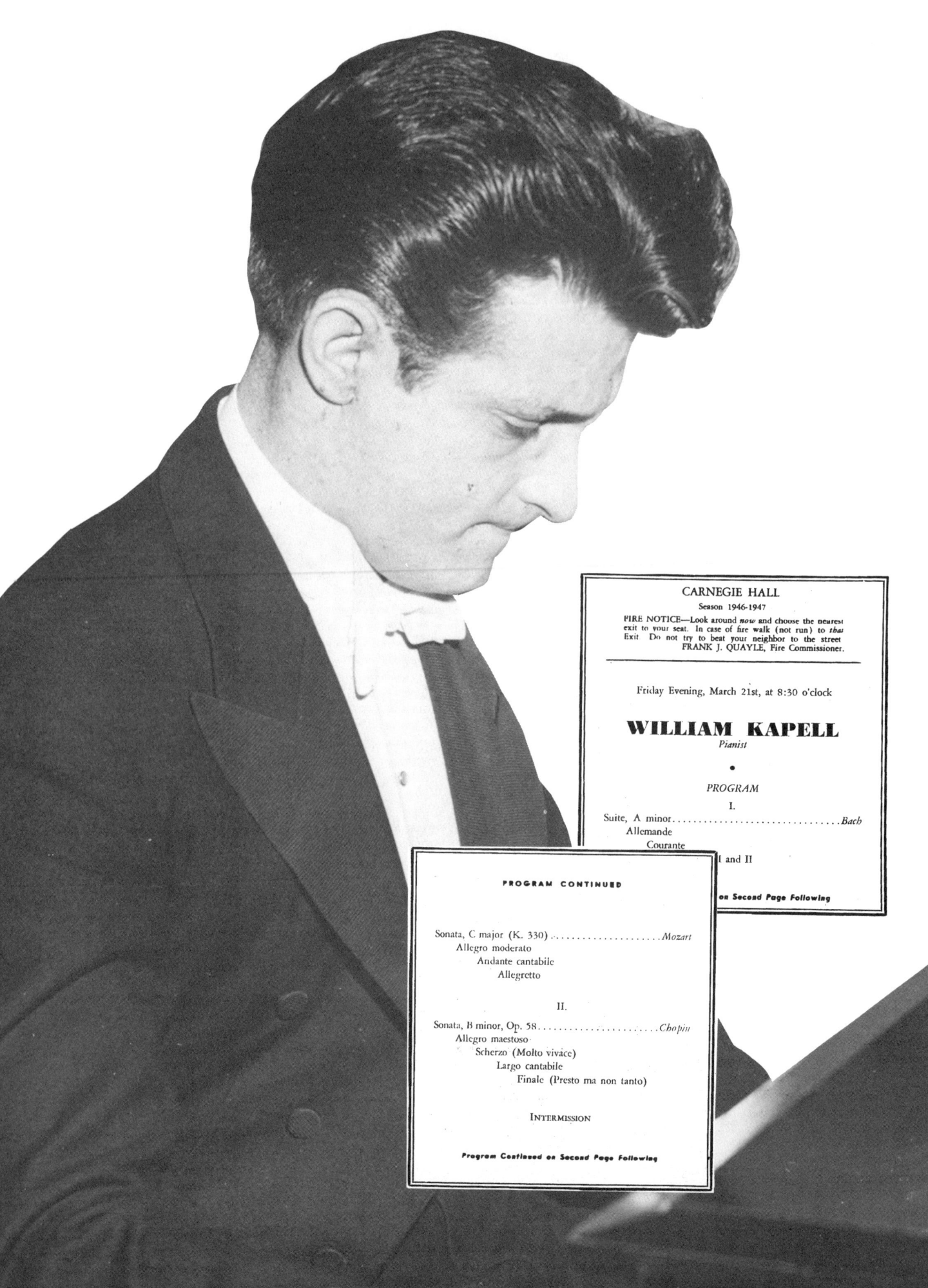

As a boy, Kapell was caught trying to sneak into Carnegie Hall. Ejected by an usher, he promised that he would be back someday, and playing on the Carnegie Hall stage. (Left) He was as good as his word — not once but many times. (Right) Kapell listens to a playback of one of his early recordings.

WILLIAM KAPELL, Pianist . . . Exclusive RCA VICTOR Red Seal Recording Artist

Arthur Rubinstein was Kapell's first musical hero, but the relationship between the pianists was often strained. They were radically different men—in their temperaments and in the way they approached their art. (Below) Laura Dubman (later Fratti) and Rubinstein, with whom she studied in Paris. She was one of Kapell's closest friends, and he admired her musicianship enormously.

Kapell met Aaron Copland during his summers in the Berkshires. The pianist usually put either the Sonata or the Piano Variations on international programs, and Copland dedicated his Piano Fantasy to Kapell's memory.

> Hotel Empire
> 63 St. & B'way
> N.Y.C.
>
> Dear Willy Kapell:
>
> It was very nice of you to write me that long letter about the Piano Sonata. I hope the piece is as good as you think it is — in which case it won't wither at all from having to wait a season for the bang-up performance that I look forward to hearing you give.
>
> All my best to you — hope we see you up the Berkshires again this summer.
>
> Yours cordially,
> Aaron Copland

Interplay

AMERICAN CONCERTETTE

FOR PIANO AND ORCHESTRA

By

MORTON GOULD

Transcribed for Two Pianos
(*The Orchestra Arranged For A Second Piano*)

In Four Movements
FIRST MOVEMENT
SECOND MOVEMENT—*GAVOTTE*
THIRD MOVEMENT—*BLUES*
FOURTH MOVEMENT

PRICE $3.50

MILLS MUSIC, INC.
1619 Broadway, New York, N. Y.

To Willy — My dearest dearest friend with love, affection, esteem, comradeship, pride, joy, sorrow, (Fill in — — — Marty

To Willy — Sincerely yours, M. Gould

As a composer, conductor, pianist, broadcaster and administrator, Morton Gould was an important figure in American music for more than half a century.

Artur Rodzinski, the conductor of the New York Philharmonic and an early admirer. (Below) Kapell struck up a close professional friendship with the severe and uncompromising Fritz Reiner, with whom he is shown during a late 40s visit to the conductor's home in Westport, Connecticut.

Composers of three continents: (above) the Brazilian Heitor Villa-Lobos; (left) the American Charles Wakefield Cadman; (right) the Armenian Aram Khachaturian.

Pages from Kapell's press book; the Keller anecdote could be adapted for any town in which the pianist played.

```
                    PRESS BOOK
                        FOR
                     PIANIST
                W I L L I A M   K A P E L L
                     CONTENTS

     1.  Biography
     2.  Kapell: Three Periods
     3.  Technique and Musicianship: an Article by Kapell
     4.  Briefs
     5.  Kapell Seeks Cream of Everything
     6.  Great Music Is National, Says Kapell
     7.  Kapell Abroad
     8.  The William Kapell Scholarship
     9.  The Old Masters of Tomorrow
    10.  Helen Keller Enjoys Kapell's Music


     To the Local Manager

         The stories in this press book should be adapted
         to fit the particular needs of your city, filled
         in with the necessary local information, and re-
         typed before releasing them to your newspapers,
         with accompanying mats, or photographs of the
         artist.  If there is anything else you need,
         please let us know.
                                   PRESS DEPARTMENT




                COLUMBIA ARTISTS MANAGEMENT, Inc.
            Personal Direction:  Judson, O'Neill and Judd
     113 West 57th Street                     New York 19, N.Y.
                       RCA Victor Records
                        Steinway Piano
```

31

From Judson, O'Neill and Judd
Publicity: WILLIAM KAPELL

-10-

HELEN KELLER ENJOYS KAPELL'S MUSIC

One snowy evening a season or so ago, just before Christmas, William Kapell, who will appear here_____ at_____, was soloist with the Philadelphia Orchestra in Constitution Hall, Washington, D.C. After he played the Rachmaninoff Second Concerto, the audience rose to its feet in an ovation. In the audience, in one of the forward boxes, sat a woman enjoying the vibrations which are her only contact with the outside world -- Helen Keller, deaf, dumb and blind.

Glenn Dillard Gunn recorded the incident in the Washington Times-Herald:

"One of the most attentive and interested witnesses of young Kapell's triumph with the Philadelphia Orchestra was Helen Keller, though how this remarkable woman, denied sight and hearing, could participate in this fine and exciting bit of music-making seems inexplicable. But participate she did, apparently with as much satisfaction as was manifested by the applause and the shouting of the multitude. She often moved a and in time to the rhythm. She smiled when the young virtuoso set forth an especially effective climax. She applauded with the rest of us; and at the intermission she asked to be conducted backstage so that she might express her congratulations."

-oOo-

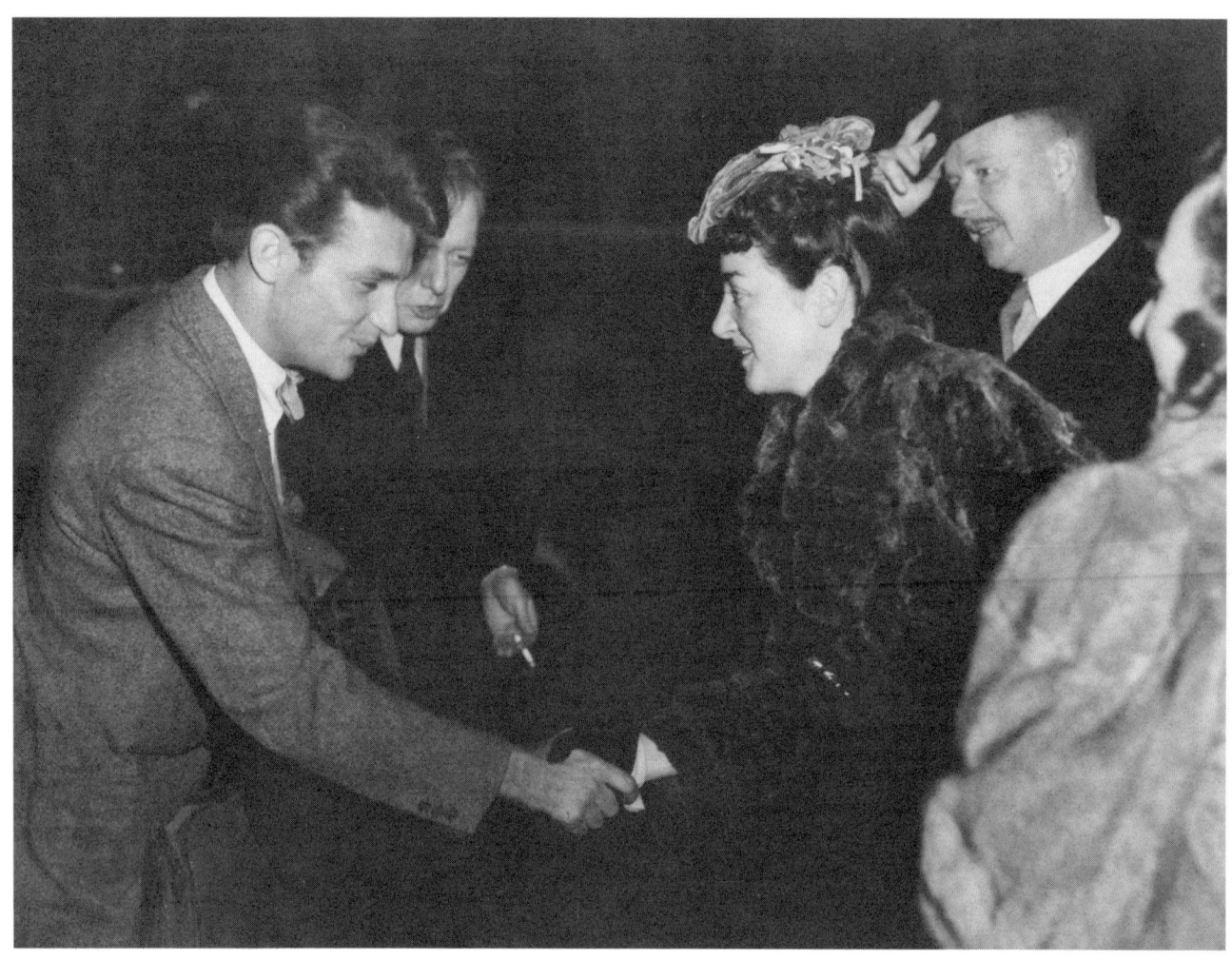

By the time he was in his mid-20s, Kapell was touring internationally — Europe, South America and Australia. The 1945 tour of Australia was in every way a triumph. (Above) He is greeted at the airport. (Right) The Australian press found the young American excellent copy.

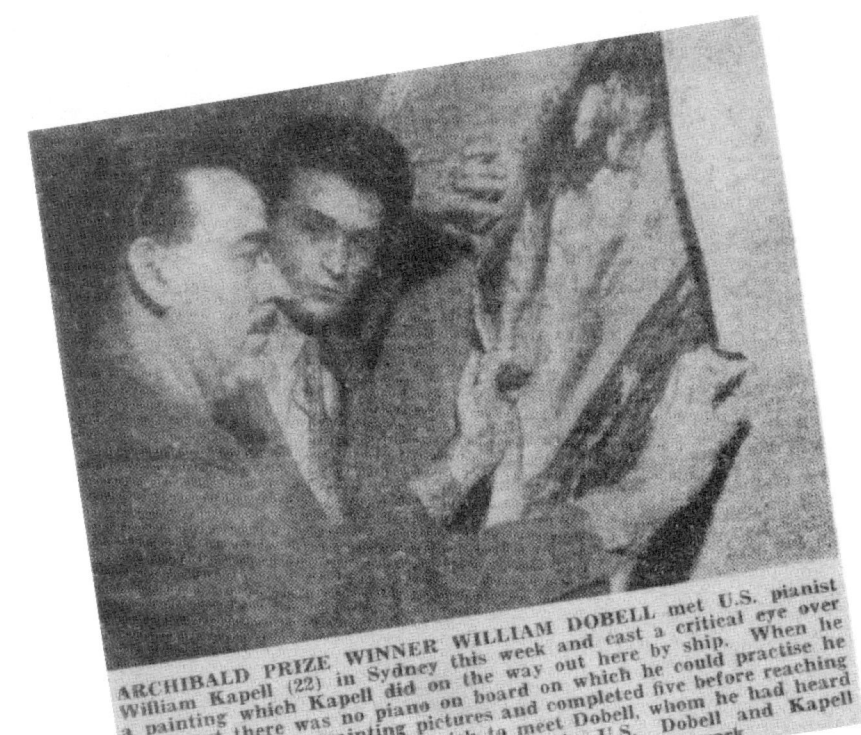

ARCHIBALD PRIZE WINNER WILLIAM DOBELL met U.S. pianist William Kapell (22) in Sydney this week and cast a critical eye over a painting which Kapell did on the way out here by ship. When he found out there was no piano on board on which he could practise he turned his hand to painting pictures and completed five before reaching Sydney. He had expressed a wish to meet Dobell, whom he had heard praised by conductor Eugene Ormandy in U.S. Dobell and Kapell agreed to exchange a copy of each other's work.

LATEST OVERSEAS ARTIST TO REACH AUSTRALIA is 22-years-old American pianist William Kapell (left), who is under engagement to the A.B.C. and opens his season in Adelaide tomorrow night. He was photographed in Sydney with another 22-years-old world renowned pianist, Noel Mewton-Wood, of Melbourne, who is at present giving a Sydney season.

Kapell with the New Zealand pianist Richard Farrell, who became something of a protege and gave signs of developing into a fine musician before his death in an automobile accident. (Above) Some music talk in Australia with the pianist Noel Mewton-Wood and the conductor Sir Malcolm Sargent.

Kapell looks less than fully engaged in this series of publicity photographs with various native creatures taken during the tour at an Australian zoo. (Below right) Young Australians wait excitedly to meet the pianist after a concert.

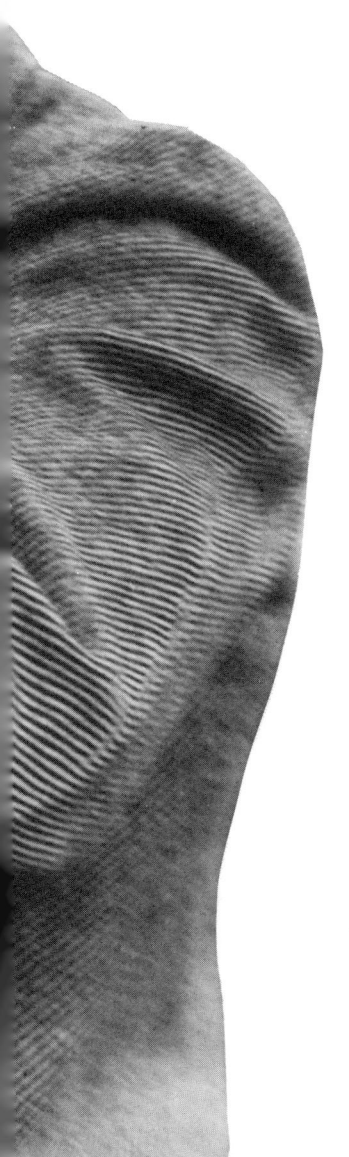

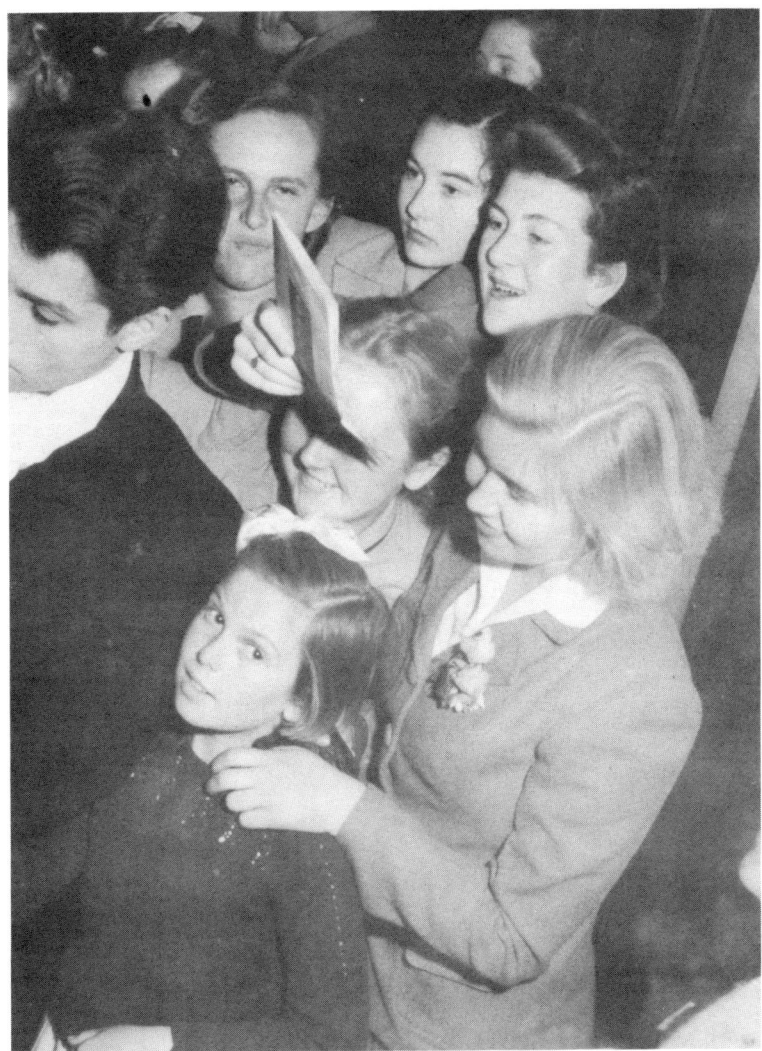

WILLIAM KAPELL

WILLIAM KAPELL is world famous far beyond his years. His "seven league boots career" has carried him back and forth across the United States and Canada the past decade and has taken him overseas to Europe, "down under" to Australia and New Zealand and three times to South America. Illuminating statistics are the facts that in this period he has played four dozen times with the Philadelphia Orchestra and has made more than three dozen appearances in the city of Chicago.

Born in New York City September 20, 1922, William Kapell studied as a child with Dorothea Anderson LaFollette; later with Olga Samaroff Stokowski who was one of the great influences in his life. Before he was twenty Kapell had won three major awards: the Youth Contest of the Philadelphia Orchestra, the Naumburg Foundation Award, and the Town Hall Endowment Award. His career was officially launched in July 1942 when he made his first appearance in New York with orchestra — at the Stadium Concerts with the Philharmonic-Symphony.

From that date to this the Kapell career has made "news" and his name has spelled fame.

"Mr. Kapell played with unlimited fire and elan ... in the grand manner. There was technique to burn, and in the performance an authority and excitement not to be resisted. A young musician of exceptional attributes was ablaze at his task."
Olin Downes, New York Times

"One of the most striking evenings of piano-playing in our memory."
New York Herald Tribune

"He possesses as formidable a technical and musical equipment as any newcomer (or old-comer), for that matter, who ever appeared with the orchestra." *Boston Herald*

"The vigor and style of a young god."
Philadelphia Record

"I went to his concert tired, I came away refreshed." *San Francisco Examiner*

"Kapell performed with towering pianistic mastery and brilliant discernment." *New York Post*

"Among the elite of the keyboard."
Philadelphia Bulletin

"The outstanding young pianist of the country. He has power, electric quality and musicianship."
Vogue

"Brought back memories of Rachmaninoff himself ... Here was flashing, sure technique; and here was overwhelming sound, produced in the grand manner." *Newsweek*

"He has the grand manner of Rubinstein and the fingers of Horowitz ... He is one of the great pianists." *Claudia Cassidy, Chicago Tribune*

Kapell's RCA VICTOR releases

Khachaturian Concerto for Piano and Orchestra with Serge Koussevitzky and the Boston Symphony
Beethoven Piano Concerto No. 2 in B-flat with Vladimir Golschmann and the NBC Symphony
Prokofieff Piano Concerto No. 3 in C with Antal Dorati and the Dallas Symphony
Rachmaninoff Piano Concerto No. 2 in C minor with William Steinberg and the Robin Hood Dell Orchestra
Rachmaninoff Rhapsody on a Theme of Paganini, Op. 41, with Fritz Reiner and the Robin Hood Dell Orchestra
Liszt "Mefisto Waltz"
Debussy Children's Corner Suite (Excerpts)
Albeniz "Evocacion"
Shostakovitch Three Preludes from Opus 34
Rachmaninoff Prelude in C Sharp Minor
Rachmaninoff Sonata in G Minor, with 'cellist Edmund Kurtz
Brahms Sonata No. 3 in D Minor, with Jascha Heifetz

COLUMBIA ARTISTS MANAGEMENT INC.
Personal Direction: JUDSON, O'NEILL & JUDD • 113 West 57th Street • New York 19, N.Y.
434 STEINWAY PIANO PRINTED IN U.S.A.

Columbia Artists printed a succession of promotional flyers for Kapell, including a photograph, a biography, some glowing press notices and a discography. Much the same formula is used to this day.

RCA Victor took out advertisements —featuring Kapell and other artists on the label — in magazines and program guides throughout the country. Although Kapell never recorded commercially with Stokowski, several private tapes exist of their collaborations together.

RECORDING EXCLUSIVELY for RCA Victor, he brings you a wealth of his greatest performances for encore after encore! Among them:

- Concerto for Piano and Orchestra, No. 2—Beethoven. With the NBC Symphony Orchestra, Vladimir Golschmann, Cond. DM-1132, $6.
- Concerto for Piano and Orchestra (1936)—Khatchaturian. With the Boston Symphony Orchestra, Serge Koussevitzky, Conductor. DM-1084, $6.
- Three Preludes from Op. 34—Shostakovich, and Prelude in C-sharp Minor —Rachmaninoff. Record 11-8824, $1.25.

ces include Federal excise tax and are subject to change without tice. ("DM" albums also available in manual sequence, $1 extra.)

thing you've wanted in nger and radio in one " tone. AM, short wave, s automatically. "Silent Victrola 612-V4. ("Vic-

RCA VICTOR Records

NE TO THE RCA VICTOR SHOW STARRING ROBERT MERRILL 2:30 P.M. SUNDAYS OVER WNEC

"Pianist of thirty fingers"

writes Oliver LaFarge about William Kapell

"In the days of Franz Liszt there appeared a cartoon which shows the fabulous virtuoso at the keyboard. He has six hands and arms. Listening to Kapell play, I have the same dizzy illusion. I am positive thirty fingers are at work. But I am positive of more than that. Sheer poetry animates those mythical fingers."
—*Oliver LaFarge*

Have you heard William Kapell play
Khatchaturian: Concerto for Piano & Orchestra
Rachmaninoff: Prelude in C Sharp Minor
Beethoven: Concerto No. 2, in B Flat

We have put together in a little book, titled "Words and Music," photographs of the world's greatest artists, together with word sketches by 36 famous authors. If you would like a copy, write RCA Victor, Record Department 205, Camden, N. J.

Kapell never mastered the trick of looking spontaneous when posing for publicity; in these pictures, he is obviously acutely aware of the camera. Constance Hope was his publicist for only a little more than a year, although she remained a friend until his death.

NATIONAL ANTHEM plagued pianist William Kapell in Victoria. He muffed "God Save the King."

'THE KING' STUMPED HIM

Lefthanded Praise On Pianist's Anthem

William Kapell is practicing up "God Save the King" like crazy for his concert here Thursday night.

The young New York concert pianist confessed today at Hotel Vancouver that he chose Victoria —of all places—to flub the venerable anthem, Tuesday night.

And he got a typical Victoria compliment for it from a dignified matron who visited him backstage.

"Y'know," she said, "it was the most original 'God Save the King' I've heard in yahrs.'

"It was the most embarrassing moment of my life," Kapell smiled today. "Peculiar things began to happen in the bass. It got worse and worse . . .

"And I forgot they don't applaud it at the end of a concert. When I finished I sat there waiting for applause. They sat there waiting for me to leave the stage . . . I finally slunk off the stage."

Soviet Attempt to Control Art 'Silly'

Kapell Says Russia Trying to Do the Impossible With Music

By RALPH DALY

Russia's effort to tell outstanding Soviet composers what kind of music to write is "a silly attempt to do something impossible."

Members of the Soviet central committee on arts who spanked eight composers in February for "a trend against the people" are displaying "a stupid political attitude and will just make fools of themselves. It is impossible for a government to control artistic expression."

So says William Kapell, 25, brilliant New York pianist who soared to the top of the concert world in five years through a piece of modern Soviet music.

NOT ONLY ONES

The shock-haired, sharp-eyed little pianist was not even slightly interested in the politics of Russian musical dictation when he discussed the problem of state control of artistic expression at Hotel Vancouver today.

He plays at the Auditorium Thursday night.

Nor did he agree with a popular theory that, even if the Soviet pushes its composers around, they are the only living men writing great music.

He thinks, in fact, that Aram Khachachurian, whose Piano Concerto Kapell put into the repertoire of major North American symphony orchestras, is writing "towards" the people just about as far as anyone could.

'HAIR RAISER'

The piano concerto like Khachachurian's juke-box-conquering "Sabre Dance," says Kapell, is "a terrific hair raiser . . . the most mass-rousing concerto of the century."

But, he asks, "would the milkman listen to it?"

Kapell agreed to perform the concerto five years ago for $75 "when no other pianist would touch it, and most my fellow students couldn't even pronounce his name (cat-cha-chur-ian)."

Celebrities were expected to be experts on everything — from local protocol to international politics. (Right) This Weegee-like candid, taken in Vancouver, catches the pianist in an unbuttoned mood, much more relaxed than he seems in most photographs taken of him.

The selling of a famous musician.

Boogie Addiction Denied By Piano Virtuoso Kapell

Since the age of 10, William Kapell, piano virtuoso, has kept his nose to the grindstone—a grindstone made up of 88 black and white keys—and he loves it.

The slight, tousle-headed musician, who will make his third local appearance with the San Antonio Symphony Orchestra Saturday evening, decided at an early age that he wanted to play the piano because "I heard other people play, and I wanted to play, too."

Kapell took his first serious pokes at the 88 keys in the family residence located above his father's New York City book store, where he was born Sept. 20, 1922, and he has been poking with increasing seriousness ever since.

Kapell's concert touring, which occupies about 10 months of every year, has taken him all over the United States, to Canada, Australia, Brazil, Argentina, Uruguay and throughout Europe.

Before he was 20, he had won three notable awards for his playing: The Youth Contest of the Philadelphia Orchestra, the Naumburg Foundation prize and the Town Hall Endowment Series award. He has played seven times with the Boston Symphony Orchestra alone. "Life," he says, "is 155 per cent piano."

Kapell's taste in music is classically catholic; he likes the works of "all great composers." Though some of his publicity material claims he plays boogie-woogie for parties, he doesn't. He does, however, have a special fondness for folk music, and attendants at Saturday night's performance may be treated to some South American folk music as Kapell's encore offerings.

Kapell's two scheduled selections for the San Antonio concert are Beethoven's Second Concerto and Rhapsody on a Theme of Paganini by Rachmaninoff.

[...] travel with the [...] Symphony Orchestra [...] he will play [...] Following [...] he will play [...] prior to his [...] he appears [...] he says, [...] work, one [...] to the [...]

Photogenic Pianist—
New Hero for Bobby-Soxers May Move Sinatra Over

William Kappel, Brilliant Concert Pianist, Latest Rage of 'Teen-Agers, to Play Here

By BETTY-JO DANIELS

The fact that he is extremely photogenic—not the fact that he is one of the youngest, most brilliant and nationally acclaimed pianists—brings bobby-soxers by the thousands to concert halls to hear him play.

They stand in herds, droves, outside the concert halls, admiring the full length color-photos of the 24-year-old William Kapell.

Wants to Lock Doors

"Everything would be all right—if only the backstage doors could be locked," Bill smiled. "But are they disappointed when they see the real product.

He recalled how in St. Louis he had "knocked himself out" during a concert and rushed backstage to mop the perspiration from his brow.

"I was standing there in my white tie and tails with a towel around my neck, completely exhausted when the left-wing door burst open and a frantic-looking young thing in short sox burst on the scene.

"She asked me if I could please tell her where to find Mr. Kapell—she had enjoyed his performance so immensely."

Private Lives

Private Lives
By Paul Ford

WINNER'S LAUREL — AT THE AGE OF TEN, PIANIST WILLIAM KAPELL WON A PIANO CONTEST. HIS PRIZE: A TURKEY DINNER WITH JOSE ITURBI AS HOST.

MR. KAPELL'S HOBBY IS PAINTING.

IT'S NOT THE humidity, it's the heat, moaned William (Willie) Kapell yesterday as he leaned against the first available piano, refusing even to smile for The Star's photographer. He had arrived in this local heat wave 24 hours ahead of schedule and was lamenting this fact. Tonight he will be playing Rachmaninoff's Second piano concerto at the Butler Bowl with Fabien Sevitzky and the Indianapolis Summer Symphony orchestra. The concert tonight will close the summer symphony series. An all-Russian program is scheduled.

William Kapell, who will give his only New York solo recital this year at Carnegie Hall on March 21, says that if he had not chosen music as his profession his second choice would have been painting. A self-taught artist, marines and landscapes in water colors and oils are his favorite subjects.

A native New Yorker, Kapell attended New York's public schools and the Columbia Grammar School. From the age of 10 to 16, Mr. Kapell studied with Mrs. Dorothea Anderson La Follette at the La Follette Music School in New York. When he was 16 he won a scholarship to the Philadelphia Conservatory of Music, where he studied under the tutelage of Mrs. Olga Samaroff Stokowski. In 1940 he entered the Julliard Graduate School on a fellowship, continuing his studies there with Mrs. Samaroff Stokowski.

Upon completion of his current concert tour, Mr. Kapell will make appearances in London, Brussels, Vienna, Rome, Stockholm, Copenhagen, Paris, Holland and Switzerland.

Kapell Likes His Beef Rare, Music Straight

By BETTY CALDWELL
Rocky Mountain News Writer

William Kapell, brilliant young pianist who will appear with the Denver Symphony Orchestra tomorrow night, is a man who likes his music straight and his roast beef very rare.

Interviewed last night while he was dining in a downtown Denver restaurant, the concert artist interspersed his comments about the "electric effect of playing for an intelligent audience" with comments about the culinary crime of putting spicy sauce on roast beef.

Five-Year Veteran at 25

A minor contretemps occurred when Kapell and the head waiter disagreed about how the meat had been cooked. The waiter said it had been roasted only in its own juices, while Kapell insisted something else had been added, "probably curry."

A veteran of five years on the concert stage though only 25, Kapell expressed his "highest regard" for Saul Caston, conductor of the Denver Symphony. Kapell appeared with him in Philadelphia.

Kapell, a native New Yorker and the first musician his family ever produced, said he feels when he walks out on the stage an "electric something" that tells him whether it is an intelligent audience.

The only way to educate audiences, he said, is to "give them the greatest," rather than play only compositions which are generally familiar.

Not Just a 'Relaxation'

"Music should be more than pleasant experience," he said. "Two hours spent at a concert person should in some way. It's a stimulation, not just relaxation like going to the...

Commenting on the criticism of José Iturbi, among purists the artist who has gone commercial, Kapell said: "He has forsaken the field—the concert stage for another, the movies.

"He is capable of great things, and he was one of the most respected artists. However, about five years he..." he has just what he will find it tough...

William Kapell

U.S. pianist Kapell looks like Sinatra

The Australian Women's Weekly

Child prodigy fulfilled his early promise

"Sinatra of the concert platform" is the name some Americans give the brilliant 22-year-old pianist, William Kapell, who is in Australia for the A.B.C.

The likeness is only in appearance. It is intensified at the end of a concert season when Kapell has lost weight and looks drawn and tired.

WILLY, as Kapell is called by intimates, has had a sensational career.

But although he began as a child prodigy, he is a modest young man.

He has an attractive, restless vitality. While he talked in Sydney he moved about the room, sometimes stopping and straddling a chair, emphasising each remark vividly with his slender hands.

His gestures are no doubt inherited from his ancestors. Although born on East Side, New York, he is of Spanish, Russian, and Polish stock.

No musical background can be traced in the Kapell family, but all have a strong appreciation of music. Willy did not begin music lessons seriously until he was ten years old, although he had shown five, when he began trying to teach himself.

Six weeks after starting lessons he entered for his first competition, one for children of New York Settlement Schools of New York...

He recalls as one of his most memorable experiences the night he was taken by Madame Stokowski to dine with the great composer at Pasadena, California.

Rachmaninoff took him after dinner to hear Horowitz playing Rachmaninoff's Third Concerto. It was a magnificent performance, and the composer listened with tears in his eyes.

"The applause was tremendous and continued for twenty minutes like heavy rain pounding on the roof," said Kapell.

"I was so ecstatic at the end that I left the hall in a daze and found myself in the wrong car."

Last year Kapell created a furore when he gave his first performance of the Piano Concerto of Armenian...

A Young ARTIST At Home

By Gladys Miller
New York City
(Author of Pleasant Homes)

WILLIAM Kapell is on a concert tour to South America, but he leaves a very attractive apartment in the States while he plays to audiences in Rio de Janiero and Buenos Aires.

The first impression you will have when you see Kapell's place is its strength and vigor. It is a masculine room. The room reflects the curiosity of the owner in the well-used books and shelves and in the original Mexican scene painted by Helen Light presented to Kapell by the artist. painting is bold and colorful and correctly placed above the mantel a very much used fireplace.

The basic colors in the room warm beige and a rich brown printed draperies introduce a sharp royal blue, but the entire rug retains the beige and brown furniture is of bleached walnut.

BOOKSHELVES ARE BUILT

Bookshelves built in on either side of the fireplace and filled to the top with books add warmth and color to the room. The various jackets of the books add...that indicates... note.

July 21, 19__

WILLIAM KAPELL, American pianist, visiting ings to William Dobell.

His next love after music is painting. The walls of his apartment on Fifth Avenue, New York, are decorated with his own work.

He has not had any lessons. "Painting is like everything else I have ever done," he said. "It seems to be pure instinct."

One of his early contacts on arrival in Australia was William Dobell, whom he was much...

William Kapell's living room features built-in bookcases and a Mexican scene painted by Helen Light.

When you read of his many achievements, you realize that regardless of age, he is a mature person.

When Kapell returns from South America, he will start a concert tour in the States, taking time out to play with the philharmonic symphony orchestra at Carnegie Hall.

This fall he is starting a scholarship fund for children from six to 12 years old. The winners will study under his teacher, Mrs. Dorothea Anderson La Follette. Mrs. La Follette seems to be as interested in young musicians as he is, for besides her regular pupils, she teaches at the Yorkville settlement.

A SIXTEEN-POUND PIANO

When Kapell left for South America he took with him on the plane a sixteen-pound piano that a friend of his designed and presented to him. This piano is revolutionary as metal alloy rods replace the strings making a lighter instrument and one not affected readily by climatic changes. This piano is not made commercially but when it is, it will be popular, as it will be less expensive, giving more children the opportunity to learn to play.

The piano is small and light and is easier to arrange, as it may be placed at right angles to the wall and the pianist may face his audience and share in their enjoyment of the music. It may be moved easily from room to room. If its musical quality is as fine, it is no wonder Kapell enjoys it.

ARTISTIC CONFERENCE.
William Kapell, young American pianist, and Artur Rodzinski, conductor of the New York Philharmonic-Symphony Orchestra, go over some points in the Khatchaturian Piano Concerto No. 3, which Kapell played with that organization on Nov. 21, 22 and 24. (Photo by Ben Greenhaus.)

Rising scales. Concert pianist William Kapell is off for a seven-week tour of South America, carrying a 16-pound practice piano to test its reactions to changes of climate and altitude. The instrument, an invention of an Air Forces veteran, is made of light materials, including aluminum and fiberglas. It has a range of three octaves, and has no strings to get out of tune. *(By Wide World)*

Kapell Brilliant In Piano Recital

If Aram Khatchatourian had anybody in mind at all in 1935, when he composed his Piano Concerto, it could not have been William Kapell, who was only 13 at the time. But it might well have been, because the work suits him perfectly. They are made for each other, this Concerto and Mr. Kapell, and the truth of that must be known to everyone in the large audience at Carnegie Hall last evening, where Artur Rodzinski conducted the regular Thursday program of the Philharmonic-Symphony.

This was virtuoso pianism of the highest order that young Mr. Kapell gave us. There was not the slightest sign of a flaw in the exciting performance and this holds for his playing, as well as that of the orchestra.

There is no piano concerto in the entire literature to equal this one in sheer energy, speed and sheer drive. What it wants is not a pianistic interpreter so much as a pilot, a stunt flier. It happens, also, to be pretty good music and, for my tastes the most attractive of the piano concertos to come out of modern Russia.

Mr. Rodzinski's program, all-Russian, included the Suite from Rimsky-Korsakoff's opera "Saltan" and the

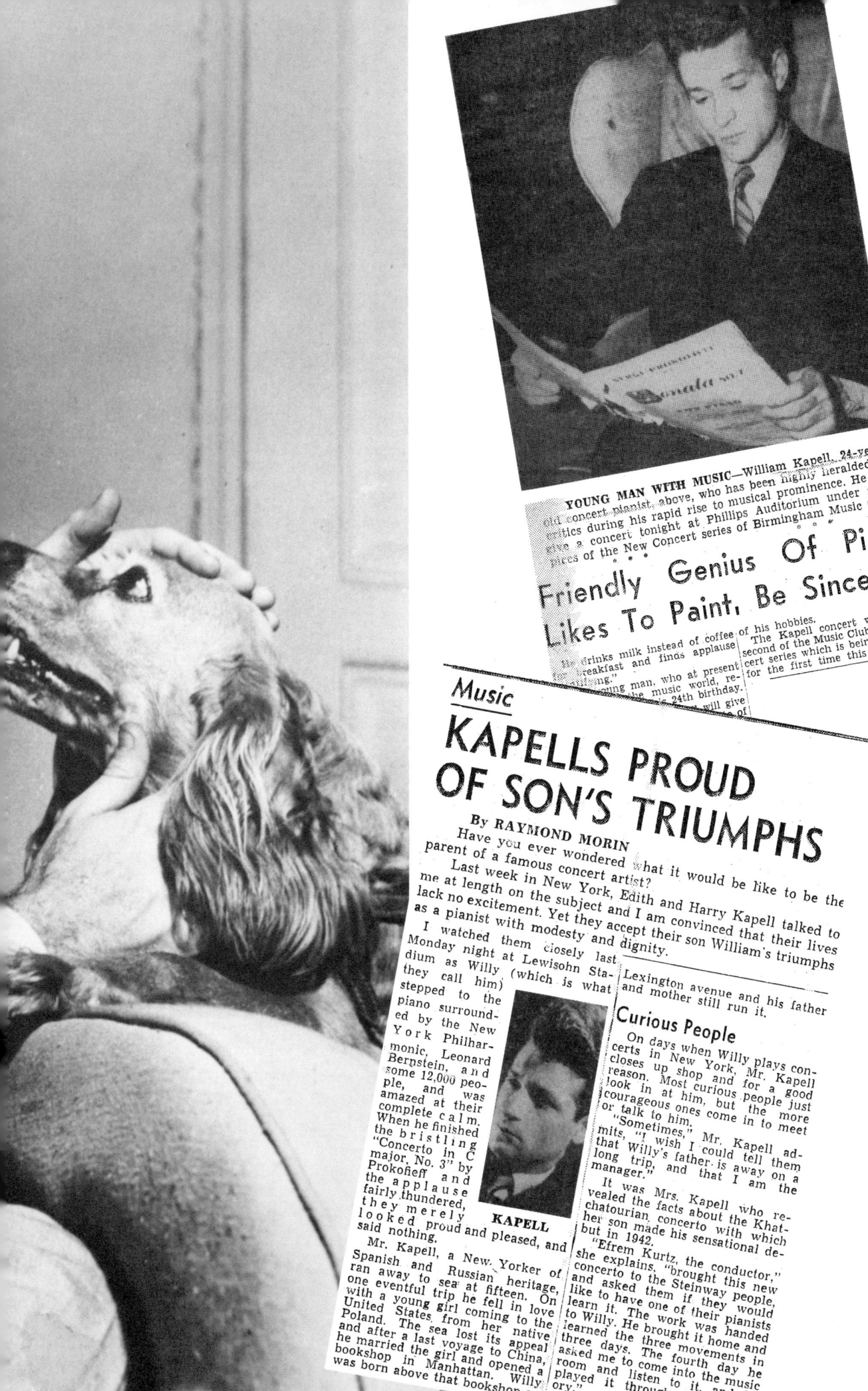

YOUNG MAN WITH MUSIC—William Kapell, 24-year-old concert pianist, above, who has been highly heralded by critics during his rapid rise to musical prominence. He will give a concert tonight at Phillips Auditorium under auspices of the New Concert series of Birmingham Music Club.

Friendly Genius Of Piano Likes To Paint, Be Sincere

He drinks milk instead of coffee for breakfast and finds applause [...] of his hobbies. The Kapell concert will be the second of the Music Club's new concert series which is being presented for the first time this year.

[...] young man, who at present [...] the music world, re-[...] 24th birthday. [...] will give [...]

Music
KAPELLS PROUD OF SON'S TRIUMPHS

By RAYMOND MORIN

Have you ever wondered what it would be like to be the parent of a famous concert artist? Last week in New York, Edith and Harry Kapell talked to me at length on the subject and I am convinced that their lives lack no excitement. Yet they accept their son William's triumphs as a pianist with modesty and dignity.

I watched them closely last Monday night at Lewisohn Stadium as Willy (which is what they call him) stepped to the piano surrounded by the New York Philharmonic, Leonard Bernstein, and some 12,000 people, and was amazed at their complete calm. When he finished the bristling "Concerto in C major, No. 3" by Prokofieff and the applause fairly thundered, they merely looked proud and pleased, and said nothing.

Mr. Kapell, a New Yorker of Spanish and Russian heritage, ran away to sea at fifteen. On one eventful trip he fell in love with a young girl coming to the United States from her native Poland. The sea lost its appeal and after a last voyage to China, he married the girl and opened a bookshop in Manhattan. Willy was born above that bookshop on Lexington avenue and his father and mother still run it.

Curious People

On days when Willy plays concerts in New York, Mr. Kapell closes up shop and for a good reason. Most curious people just look in at him, but the more courageous ones come in to meet or talk to him.

"Sometimes," Mr. Kapell admits, "I wish I could tell them that Willy's father is away on a long trip, and that I am the manager."

It was Mrs. Kapell who revealed the facts about the Khatchatourian concerto with which her son made his sensational debut in 1942.

"Efrem Kurtz, the conductor," she explains, "brought this new concerto to the Steinway people, and asked them if they would like to have one of their pianists learn it. The work was handed to Willy. He brought it home and learned the three movements in three days. The fourth day he asked me to come into the music room and listen to it, and he played it through f[...]

KAPELL

73

24 WEST 55TH STREET
NEW YORK 19

March 26, 1947

Dear Willy:

It was truly a wonderful experience last night to hear your records and to realize the big step forward you have taken in the direction you most needed progress, namely, tone. Never lose that beautiful voice again. If you listen every minute and ask it of yourself and <u>realize that you know how</u> your playing will always have this quality which is so rare and so necessary to great music.

I want to wind up our various discussions during the past ten days with the following thoughts: You spoke last night, and believe me I appreciated it deeply, of the "concept" I had given you of the Chopin Sonata and various other works. I am happy you feel that way, and yet as a teacher with long experience and a certain intuitive insight which I believe has enabled me to get the results I have gotten with talents of such different types, I want to point out to you that these concepts of single compositions are by far the <u>least</u> I have given you. Without your being fully aware of it throughout the years you have absorbed the things that every interpreter needs and the things that make a pianist an artist.

1. The capacity to recognize in a score the essence of the music.
2. A sense of form, *including harmonic structure plus feeling*
3. A sense of phrasing, *including different levels!*
4. A clarified concept of different types of touch, i.e., legato, staccato, portamento, and non-legato, *especially the rightly fingered true legato line.*
5. The reality of a dynamic scheme ranging from a triple pianissimo to a triple fortissimo, *and the pedalling that is so all-important to sound*
6. The various degrees of accents ranging from the strong beat of the bar to a double sforzando.
7. How to find tempo through the application of whatever indication the composer gives to the pulse unit in the bar.
8. The capacity to recognize the <u>significance</u> of all these printed things which so many people either ignore or take for granted.
9. The realization that every artist must be able to go beyond the printed page through imagination, instinct and capacity for emotion.
10. A method of work that insures memory and mastery. The kind of work that achieves not just notes but the way the notes should be played so that the player is not wasting a major part of his life establishing the habit of playing music the way he does not intend to perform it.
11. A sense of ensemble which was developed in you primarily through your second piano playing of concertos and which has made you an outstanding ensemble soloist with orchestras.
12. The road to enrichment of the mind through reading and outside experiences which are absolutely necessary if an artist is not to be egocentric, ingrowing and limited as a human being.

Believe me, Willy dear, <u>these</u> things are infinitely more important than any concept of any single piece. Probably any teacher would claim the teaching of these big basic things in music but the ability to make them significant to the student is apparently rare because hardly any student comes to me with such concepts in any clarified form. It is only through a constant insistence on the part of the teacher for <u>independent work</u> that finally develops in the student the capacity to handle these things himself. If there is any secret to my teaching I believe this is it. The above mentioned things are those that will enable you to go forward indepently all your life into the study of all kinds of music because, as I said to you last night, style really lies in the way the music is written and our <u>understanding</u> of all the elements that go to make it up is the thing that will enable us to approach <u>any</u> style with sureness. It is valuable to know traditions and God knows we have enough opportunity to do that through reading, listening to records, performances at concerts, etc., etc., but the only traditions that have real value are those that make the music live as the composer intended it should be. The fact that my big pupils, by that I mean pupils of big talent, are able to go on growing after they leave me as Tureck has, as Battista is doing, as you are doing, proves that this way of teaching plants the seeds for a whole artistic future.

A teacher who only provides a limited repertory of coached or imitative interpretations gives the student the easiest way to an immediate result but limits him terribly in his independent approach to a wide field.

With regard to your program for next year, I would hate to see you play the Bach-Liszt Fantasy and Fugue. These noisy transcriptions of Bach organ music are terribly dated and will re-stamp you, if one can use such a word, in the type-cast direction many people are inclined to attribute to your work. Also, as I said last night, I truly believe that the new music you take up at this point beginning work on it at a much higher level than you had before will produce wonderful results. It will mean hard work but as you seem fit it seems to me this is the right time to undertake a flight into the unknown and see what you can do with things that are in no way influenced by the various phases you have gone through during the past six years.

Good luck to you and "knock them cold" in Chicago.

Yours devotedly,

"*Madam*".

OS:ab

P.S. It is the knowledge of what you possess <u>basically</u> that gives me such confidence in your ever-growing capacities as an artist. Never forget or neglect any of them - They form the musical treasures you and I piled up together.

Despite all of the time Kapell now reluctantly devoted to public relations, he continued to grow as a musician. Samaroff remained devoted to him and sent him long letters brimming with advice.

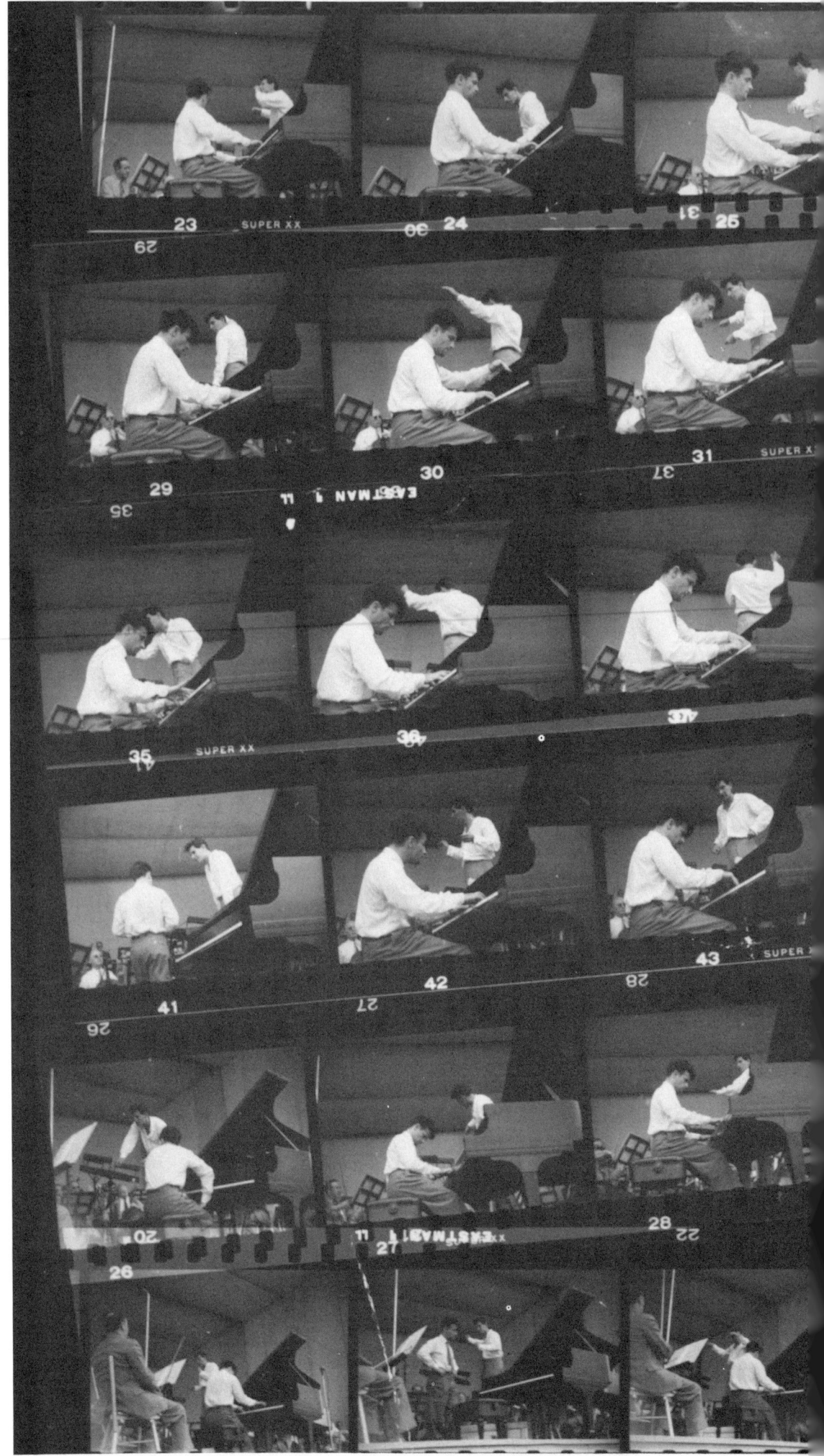

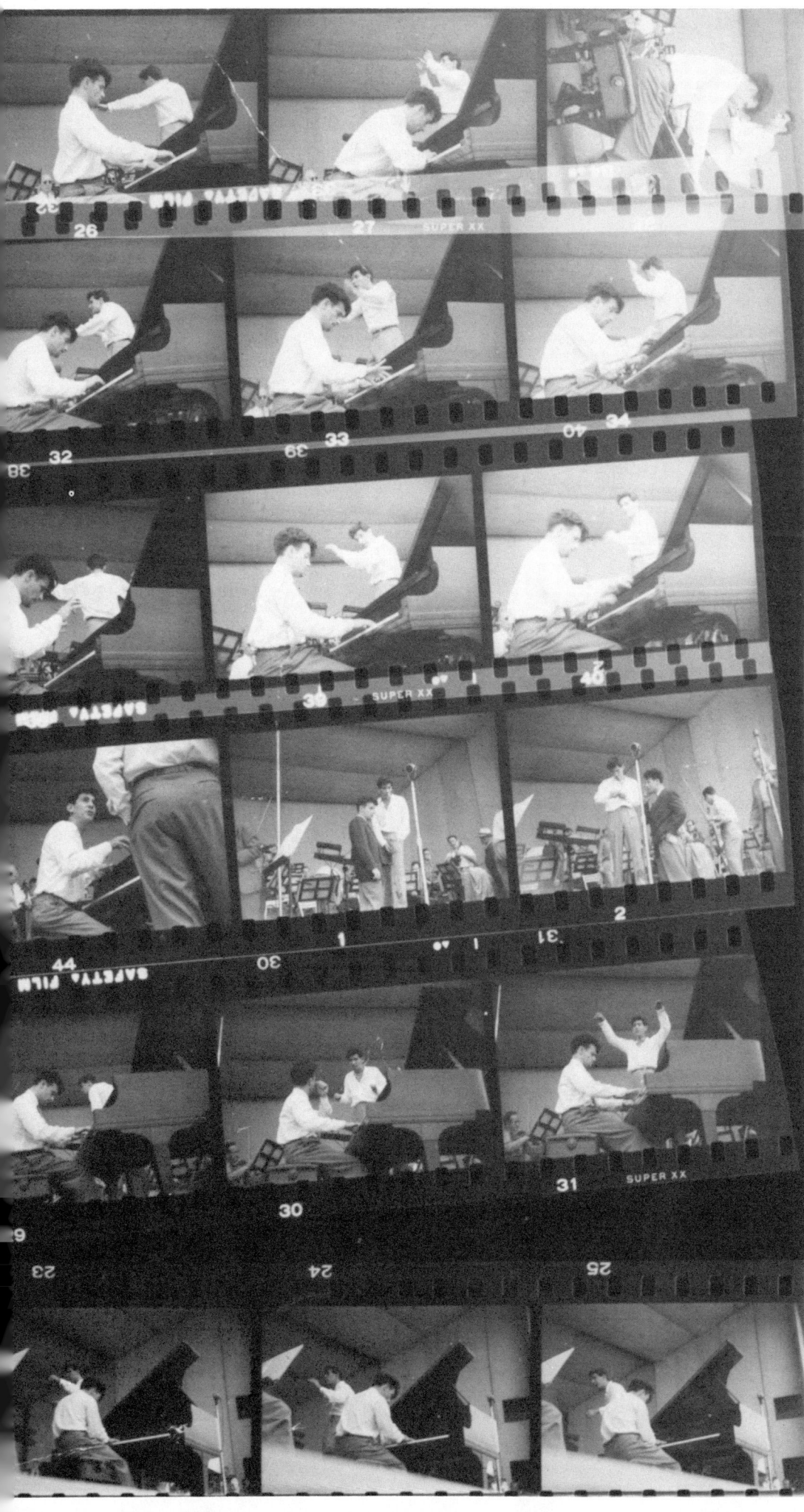

Of all the young musicians of Kapell's generation, perhaps only Leonard Bernstein matched the pianist in drive and charisma. This series of photographs was taken by Ruth Orkin at rehearsals for a performance of the Prokofiev Piano Concerto No. 3 at Lewisohn Stadium in New York.

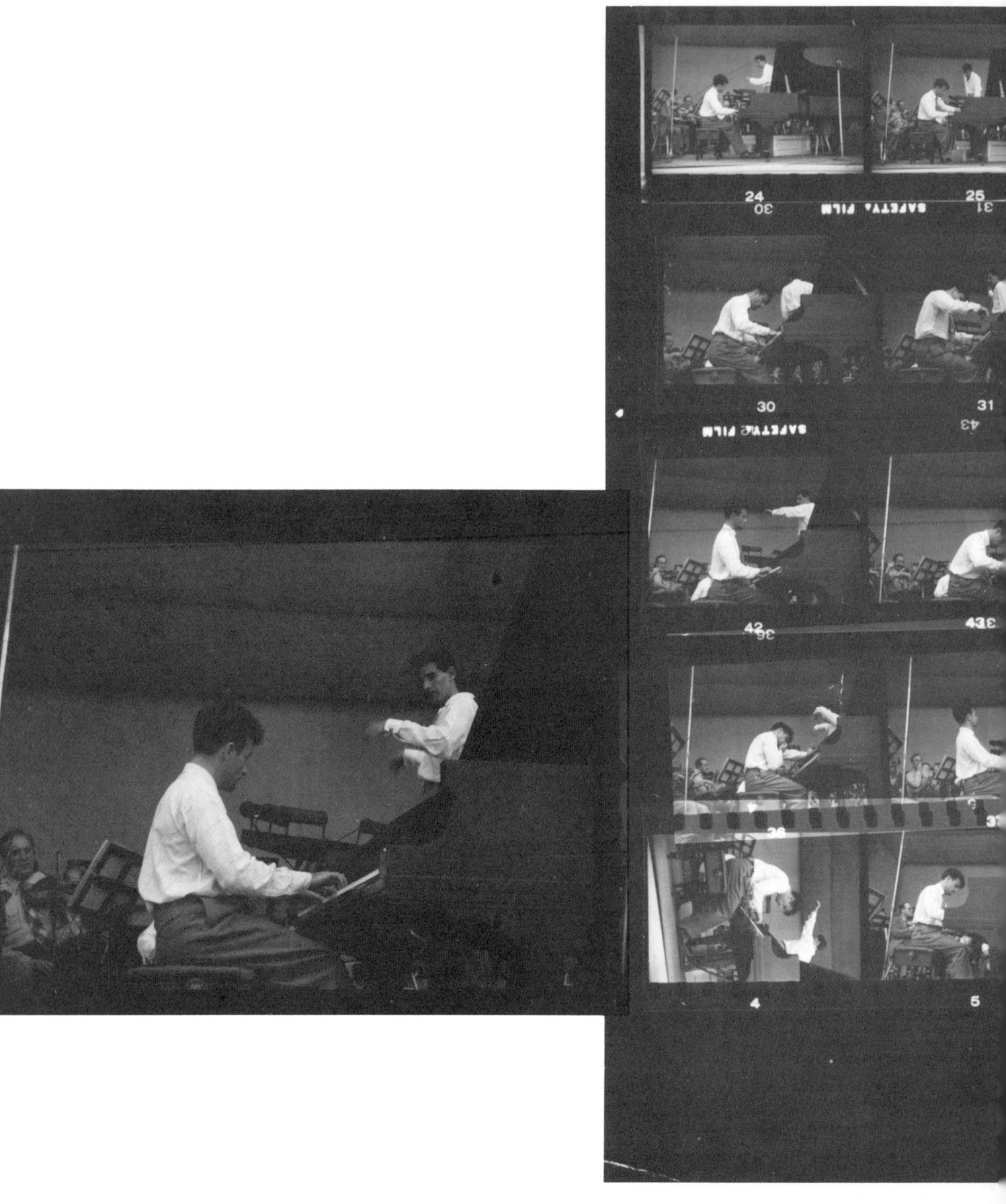

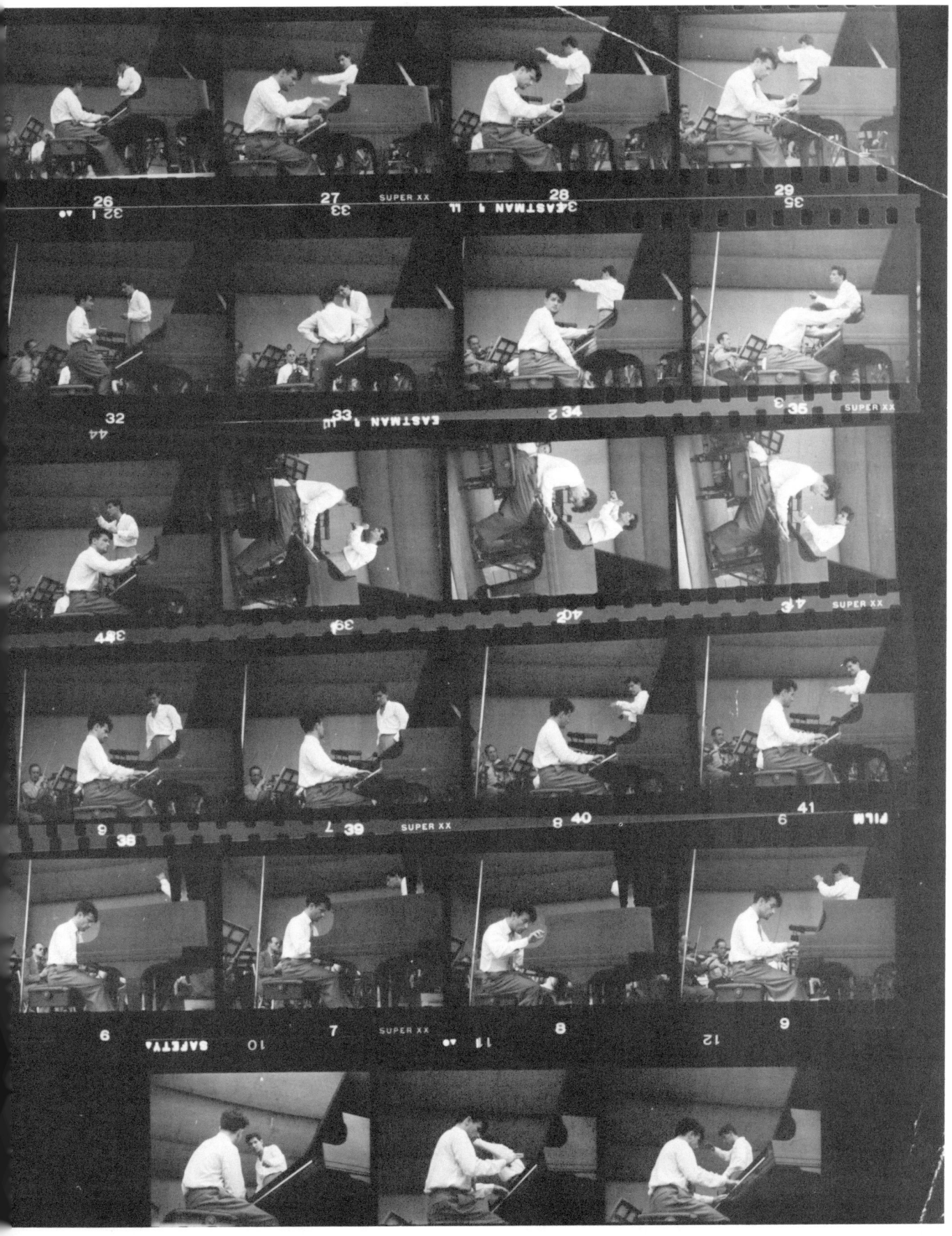

Kapell Wins Praise With Piano Recital

By ARTHUR LOESSER
Music Critic

Pianist William Kapell, who has appeared here previously as soloist with orchestra in some pyrotchnical concertos, was heard yesterday afternoon at Music Hall in a full length recital. The event was one of the National Concert Series managed by G. Bernardi.

The program ranged through a great variety of musical styles giving ample opportunity to inspect Kapell's truly impressive talents from all sides.

Judged from the point of view of pianism, Kapell's abilities must be considered as of the very highest order. On such counts as speed, strength and accuracy, control of tone and shading, emotional capacity and sense of dramatic and projective values, he can be classed with the foremost practitioners now before the public.

It may be that advancing maturity and deeper experience will help to improve his musicianly judgment in a few ways. His playing of Mozart's C major Sonata, K. 330, delightful indeed, might have been even a little more so had the slow movement been taken just a bit more flowingly.

He played Chopin's B minor Sonata magnificently, and some day he may feel that he can achieve full romantic exuberance in the first movement without an occasional lapse into harshness, and that he can realize filmy swiftness in the Scherzo without forgetting that sometimes the hand is quicker than the ear. But how could he ever improve on some of the exquisitely imaginative effects he produced in the Largo, or on the fiery sweep with which he imbued the finale?

He opened with Liszt's transcription of Bach's G minor organ Fantasy and Fugue. He realized some of the music's original grandeur and architectural cogency, without however making us regret that this kind of pianistic translation is now out of style.

On the other hand he let us enjoy three of Mendelssohn's Songs Without Words without any reservations whatsoever.

He finished with Prokofiev's Sonata No. 7. It was done with tremendous muscular energy, impressive by sheer impact and quantity of sound. Yet somehow this work does not improve on further acquaintance. Its cracks seem less than wise, its humor is brutal rather than witty. The finale is full of loud monotonous irregularity, which seems to be one of the not quite newest ideas.

Applause was hearty on the part of an audience that seemed small for the hall. Kapell played several encores.

FRIDAY, NOVEMBER 22, 1946.

KAPELL PLAYS NEW CONCERTO

By HAROLD C. SCHONBERG.

The Khatchatourian Piano Concerto, which was played last night in Carnegie Hall by William Kapell and the New York Philharmonic, is a harmless enough piece. The Armenian composer apparently knows a Russian Hollywood, where he has learned sound effects and all. He has hitched a ride on the folk-song bandwagon and whales lustily on his toy drum. Sometimes the results are pleasant, but never is there the intellectual or impressionistic synthesis of folk material that Bartok, say, achieved.

This concerto, actually, is not representative of Khatchatourian's better side. It is quite empty, with Liszt in the pianist's right hand, Rachmaninoff in his left, and an inconsistent orchestral part that has little to do with either. The composer has drawn heavily on the Oriental Armenian melos, swathing those exotic scales in an orchestral coat of many colors. There is, of course, nothing like skillful orchestration to cover a lack of essential musical ideas.

Kapell played the difficult piano part with thunderous bravura, vigor and enthusiasm. Sometimes vigor became noise, but at least he took command of the orchestra and bestrode the climaxes. His articulation is clear, he runs up a pretty set of interlocked octaves, and technically he is as efficient as a riveting machine.

The concert opened with a suite from Rimsky-Korsakoff's "Tsar Sultan," an opera known today primarily because it contains the "Flight of the Bumble Bee." It is a fine, sonorous orchestral showpiece, which served to display Rodzinski's precise way of handling tonal mass and, incidentally (in the "Bumble Bee"), the sharp, rather edgy string tone of the Philharmonic. Tschaikowsky's Fifth Symphony, a favorite of the conductor, closed the program.

Kapell also received more serious attention from the press, as the following sampling of his reviews demonstrates. Some of the most rewarding notices were those written by musicians themselves, such as the pianist Arthur Loesser in Cleveland, the composer Cecil Effinger in Denver and the composer and critic Virgil Thomson in New York.

WORDS & MUSIC
By John K. Sherman

Dorati Presents Mozart That Really Is Mozart!

THAT BOYISH, steel-fingered pianist with the bushy hair, William Kapell, was soloist with the Minneapolis Symphony orchestra last night, but I'll have to record that going back to the office I was saying to myself "What an orchestra!" and "What conducting!"

Antal Dorati had his boys and girls in the pink last night. If you wanted to hear a Mozart symphony played better than the C major, No. 34, was played, you would have to go far and wait long. This opened the bill and was really the gem of the evening.

The strings outstone themselves in this work, attaining some of the cleanest, most precise tone and technique that they've given us. And Dorati outdid himself in his revelation of Mozart as a composer who could say everything music can say with grace, wit and illumination.

This interpretation had life and eagerness all within the frame of Mozart's formalism. The melancholy of the slow movement achieved poignancy without once disturbing its basic composure. The mischievous, headlong finale was pure incandescent spirit — truly a virtuoso performance, with the violins playing with inspired agility and accuracy.

The other all-orchestral offering was at the opposite pole from Mozart and was more pictorially exciting—the three Sea Interludes from Benjamin Britten's opera, "Peter Grimes." These descriptive sketches, redolent of the sea and the fishing village which is the opera's locale, reached a swirling, shrilling climax in the storm episode, and again displayed the orchestra as a virtuoso instrument.

Kapell worked in contrasts last night too. His first appearance was in the Mozart G major concerto, No. 17, and his showpiece at concert's end was the Rachmaninoff Rhapsody on a Theme of Paganini.

His Mozart performance might be designated as a very "white" one, with cameo phrasing, a dry, even tone, an approach impersonal and objective to a fault. It was a beautifully tailored conception but lacking humanity and warmth, two qualities you can give Mozart without smearing him with the brush of romanticism. A little more expressiveness wouldn't have jarred the concerto out of the 18th century.

As for the Rachmaninoff Rhapsody, this was pianistic enginering of amazing lights and strength, like a bridge made of aluminum. Kapell's playing here was light-fingered, vigorous and "dry". His piano was percussive, rarely singing, his manner mechanistic and hardly romantic at all, and if Rachmaninoff isn't made romantic, where are you?

The result was a curiously jerky, barking production which missed a good deal of the tonal glow and grandeur that is Rachmaninoff. Without that, even so, we heard some phenomenal piano technique, with runs and scampering figures negotiated with weird velocity and precision.

William Kapell Displays Fine Musicianship in Piano Recital

By LUTHER ROWSEY

William Kapell gave eloquent proof of instinctive musicianship in a keyboard performance of dramatic intensity at the Music Hall Tuesday night.

Playing for members of Edna W. Saunders' Civic Community Concert association and patrons of her piano course, the long-haired and moodily-mannered young artist put truly romantic coloring in his recital.

Kapell exposes subtleties otherwise not found and gives a depth of meaning to compositions which are often just performed. He chose a large work from each school—classic, romantic and modern, and proceeded to display his gifts in each.

In Mozart's Sonata in C Major, the pianist shaded the delicate passages in tones of exquisite timbre, especially the andante cantabile. It was virtually sung.

Kapell gave Chopin's Sonata in B Minor a poetic delivery, one with both vigor and tenderness. In contrast with the dark and plaintive largo movement, the finale was fired with energies.

Prokofieff's Sonata No. 7, presumably the sort of thing the Russian government has found meaningless, was made quite exciting at times by the visiting pianist. Whatever its message, it was given a crisply bright and forceful sounding.

The Fantasia and Fugue in G Minor, by Bach-Liszt, was strangely stirring as handled by Kapell. Many colors were produced in a finely balanced execution. There was a very lyric line in Mendelssohn's Three Songs Without Words, and the one in F-Sharp Minor was especially charming.

Kapell's playing was not without flaws and there were times when his emotion seemed extreme or overdone, but it was something to hear and remember, nonetheless.

Kapell Charming at Piano, but More Abandon Is Needed

BY HERBERT ELWELL

William Kapell was heard in a piano recital yesterday afternoon at Public Music Hall, appearing under the auspices of the National Concert Series. The audience was not large, but it was strongly articulate in expressing its liking for the work of this gifted young American artist.

As on former occasions, he displayed a prodigous technical equipment, a keyboard facility that enables him to do whatever he wishes. And what he wishes to do is conditioned by taste and the instincts of a serious, well trained musical mind. His attitude toward the music he plays seems to be that of great respect, and this is certainly not a reprehensible thing, but it sometimes leads to overcautiousness where more abandon, depth of tone and variety of color are called for.

He also has a way of lingering over soft lyric passages, as if in a star-gazing trance. It is all charming and intimate, and the almost inaudible pianissimo passages draw one on to listen with rapt attention. But it becomes an end in itself, and one loses the direction and structural purpose of the composition.

Outstanding in his somewhat long program was the final Sonata No. 7 of Prokofieff. In this sort of slapstick bravado with its somewhat incongruous admixture of mooning romanticism, Kapell excels and lets the piano ring with scintillating surface play. It is distressing, incidentally, to find so distinguished a composer as Prokofieff being satisfied with so undistinguished a theme as that of the Andante.

Kapell began with a well organized performance of the Bach-Liszt Fantasia and Fugue in G minor. There was something delightfully personal about his Mozart Sonata in C major, K. 330. Its pinpoint dynamics almost resulted in overrefinement. Nice clarity of inner voices was to be noted in all his work, but a little too much affectation seemed to be wasted on certain modulatory chords and cliches in the Chopin B minor Sonata. The rather effeminate wooing of emotion from these sources could profitably have been balanced by something more robust.

The three Mendelssohn Songs Without Words could have been dispensed with, for they contributed little to a program already long and overburdened with romantic slow movements.

Music

Bernstein, Kapell Team Up In Brilliant Outdoor Concert

By LOUIS BIANCOLLI.

Two of the country's top musical talents teamed up in brilliant style at the Stadium last night, when Leonard Bernstein, with the Philharmonic, with William Kapell as piano soloist. A crowd estimated at 12,000 attended.

The combined gifts of Messrs. Bernstein and Kapell were heard in a terrific rendering of Prokofieff's Third Piano Concerto, a score evidently planned for the speed and vigor of youth.

While Mr. Bernstein paced the orchestra in gripping fashion, young Kapell flew through the hail of notes with a nonchalance that made one of the toughest concertos on record sound like child's play.

Dynamic Note Stressed.

The dynamic note was stressed by both. Rhythms slashed by in clipped precision, and where Prokofieff asked for an icy glitter of color the boys gave it to him.

If Mr. Kapell was one virtuoso at the keyboard, Mr. Bernstein was a second one on the podium —with the orchestra tagging along as a collective third in its own right.

For the Prokofieff concerto is so closely knit in a kind of round-robin shift of emphasis that soloist, conductor and orchestra carry on on equal terms.

The Prokofieff Concerto was part of an all-Russian program featured by Mr. Bernstein to open his short engagement as Stadium conductor, the other numbers being the "Lieutenant Kijé Suite" and Tschaikowsky's "Pathetic."

about Tschaikowsky's "Pathetic" Symphony last night was the way the airliners snuffed out the beautiful fadeout at the end.

CRESTON IS LAUDED FOR 2D SYMPHONY

Composer Acclaimed as Work Is Played by the Philadelphia Orchestra—Kapell Soloist

NOV. 22, 1946.

By OLIN DOWNES

There were brilliant offerings at the concert of the Philadelphia Orchestra under Eugene Ormandy's direction last night in Carnegie Hall. Paul Creston's Second Symphony, heard for the second time in this city and the first at the Philadelphia Orchestra's concerts, had a remarkable success. This score was introduced here by Dr. Rodzinski and the Philharmonic-Symphony Orchestra last season. It was then generally approved, but not received with the acclaim bestowed last night upon symphony and composer, who bowed from the stage.

One reason for this doubtless lies in the fact that many in the audience had heard the work once already, and were that much nearer a grasp of its qualities. Another reason, and a curious one, may also have had to do with the high level of receptivity that was demonstrated. Those who heard it for the second time may not have found it necessary to read over again the analysis of the work by the composer, contained in the program book.

For this analysis, which reads like a blueprint of some engine or turbine or electric-magneto combination, is calculated to lead the listener to expect music of the same sort. And the symphony does begin severely, if not didactically. Fortunately, the music begins to accumulate, to take charge of the situation, and run away with the more or less abstract ideas.

We have been thoughtfully informed, by the composer, that this symphony is intended as a two-fold apotheosis of song, in the first part, and dance, in the second. "Song" in the first half has reminiscences of a few composers, like Tchaikovsky, and more modern minds. "Dance" is becoming the American in traces of jazz and its concomitants. What actually happens is a score that has color, lyricism, rythmic impulsion and brilliant instrumentation. It may have this or that derivation; it may or may not precisely realize its author's structural intention. He has written an interesting and entertaining symphony. That is what fundamentally matters. And so, in the words of the prophet, what?

There was another brilliant success at this concert. It was William Kapell in his performance of the Third Piano Concerto of Prokofief. He ignited it! The music is electrical. It would give Prokofieff a significant place in modern art if he were only a temperament and not a composer at all!

The concerto is superbly assured, audacious, sometimes sardonic. It has also a special exoticism. Orchestra and piano vie with each other, playing with the ideas as capriciously and wantonly as a cat with a mouse. Nothing is impossible, in the sense of technique or effect, and the greatest extravagances are committed with a grin and a tongue in the cheek.

Mr. Kapell played with unlimited fire and elan, with a tone that sometimes became hard, but which, even in this, matched in a way the music's glitter and insolence. The piano part is a tour de force. There was technique to burn, and in the performance an authority and excitement not to be resisted. A young musician of exceptional attributes was ablaze at his task.

The orchestral pieces were excellently chosen for the occasion. Mr. Ormandy began with the fine set of Brahm's Variations on the Haydn theme and ended with an uncommonly sensitive presentation of the second "Firebird" Suite of Stravinsky. There is no music like it, in Stravinsky's scores or those of any other composer. When he wrote this music, also derivative in minor ways that do not matter, Stravinsky was a genius and a poet, with a heart that was young. The imagination, tenderness and glamour of this early score are imperishable; they never fail to move the listener when they are heard as Mr. Ormandy and his orchestra communicated them. Conductor and orchestra had reason to congratulate themselves on the evening's results.

CHICAGO DAILY TRIBUNE:

Kapell Plays Rachmaninoff Interestingly

Concert by the Chicago Symphony orchestra, Hans Lange, conductor; William Kapell, pianist. Presented in Orchestra hall Thursday evening, Nov. 23, 1944, and scheduled for repetition Friday afternoon. The program:

Symphony in E flat major for strings, two oboes and two horns .... Johann Stamitz
Concerto for Piano, No. 2, C minor .... Rachmaninoff
"In a Summer Garden" .... Delius
Tone Poem, "Don Juan" .... Strauss

BY CLAUDIA CASSIDY.

[Reprinted from yesterday's late Tribune.]

Hans Lange made his first appearance of the Chicago Symphony orchestra season at the Thanksgiving concert at Orchestra hall, with William Kapell as his soloist, playing Rachmaninoff's Second concerto to mark his downtown debut. This is the intense little 22 year old pianist with the beautiful hands and the crisp black pompadour, who had such a Ravinia success two summers ago with the contemporary work he played so often he said people were beginning to call him Willie Khachatourian Concerto.

Altho Mr. Kapell is one of the most gifted of the younger pianists—I know of no one but Leonard Pennario to rival him, unless it is the young Fleischer who played with Monteux in New York the other day—it is not yet quite time to change that middle nickname to Rachmaninoff. The C minor concerto covers a huge Russian canvas and Mr. Kapell lacks the pianistic maturity to fill in all its splendors. The great sweep of the score eludes him, and the titanic fury of its climaxes. But in the smaller scale of his own performance he played superbly, with incisive brilliance and complete musical security, and when it came to the poetry, ah, that was when Mr. Kapell shone.

Here he had the dreamy, nostalgic languor that is the very essence of the music, an almost liquid lyricism that gave the adagio the undulating cadence that is uniquely Rachmaninoff, and uniquely satisfying, if you happen to find Rachmaninoff, as some of us do, and not merely an outmoded decadent, as others do. Altho there was never a time when Kapell's hands did not seem utterly at home on the keys, in the slow movement they lived there, and the music seemed to flower beneath them. We can all wait for a talent like that to reach its full realization.

It would be a pleasure to say that the accompaniment was the magnificent Rachmaninoff long an Orchestra hall tradition, but the fact is that the orchestra did not play well Thursday night. If it will forgive me for saying so it seemed rather like a horse long accustomed to going full speed ahead under the whip, suddenly finding that it couldn't run under supple reins. It had a dispirited, lackadaisical air, and the amount of tone it achieved was scarcely in proportion to its size.

The nearest it came to giving Mr. Lange the performance he once could have taken for granted was in Delius' "In a Summer Garden," which had resilience and texture. Stamitz's symphony was cleanly but listlessly played, the Rachmaninoff simply could not achieve the old molten fusion once so exciting a part of concertgoing, and Strauss' "Don Juan" was a skeleton of its old self, tho toward the end the orchestra made a valiant effort to salvage its sagging reputation.

ON THE AISLE

Kapell's Superb Chopin Sonata Crowns Glowing Orchestra Hall Recital

BY CLAUDIA CASSIDY

THERE WAS A MAN in Orchestra hall last night who had gone to hear the "brilliant" William Kapell, and he was what you might reasonably call thunderstruck. Not just by brilliance, tho there was virtuosity and to spare. But somehow he hadn't known that Mr. Kapell, who is every day of 27, is already one of the great pianists. He hadn't known that he plays magical Mozart and monumental Bach, and that if his B minor Sonata is a Chopin sample, he has the grand manner of Rubinstein and the fingers of Horowitz.

A large order? I agree. But I am not the man who went to Orchestra hall last night to hear the "brilliant" William Kapell. I did that years ago, and decided when he played a Brahms sonata that he had not just brilliance, but the deep roots of lyricism and poetry and that quality you simply can't define, for it is an inner, blazing fire. I thought then Mr. Kapell had the makings of magnificence. I know it now.

He doesn't make a very imposing entrance. And when he sits down at the piano, he fidgets. But suddenly he plunges like a diver into his element, and begins to play. And what he plays is not just one kind of music in which he happens to specialize, but the treasures of the repertory, at polar extremes of the pianistic range. He can do this, and keep on doing it, because he has what it takes for the big time—enormous talent, an agile and inquisitive mind, not a little introspective, and the willingness not just to work, but to slave.

Like the most gifted of his generation, whether it is Leonard Bernstein, Margot Fonteyn, or Nora Kaye, he approached classicism thru romanticism, which seems to be an interesting direction. His Bach [the Liszt transcription of the Fantasy and Fugue in G minor] was stated in monumental terms, but in living tone, not granite, so that the voices of the fugue grew naturally from the big design. His Mozart, the enchanting Sonata in C Major, K. 330, was free and fresh and radiant, because he doesn't confuse depth with dissection, or mistake Scarlatti's tone for Mozart's.

That he played Prokofieff's Seventh Sonata superbly could have surprised no one familiar with his work, tho the romanticism of the work is deeper than before and the fury of the finale was polished to a rapier glitter. The Mendelssohn songs without words were as charmingly sung as the Schumann encore, but for me, the crown of the recital was that Chopin.

How Kapell has gone forward you might have guessed when he readjusted his program, moving the Prokofieff before intermission and putting the Chopin last. For where the Prokofieff was scintillant, the Chopin was magnificent. It was all of a piece, even the elusive largo. It was deep and glowing in tone, spacious in design, headlong but superbly controlled in execution. The wonderful opening flung out the challenge, the feathery fleetness of the turn and the virtuosity of the triumphant finale carried it to triumph. Mr. Kapell is still going places. But by grace of a quirk in the language we can also say that he has arrived.

Kapell Masters Difficult Concerto

By CECIL EFFINGER
Denver Post Music Editor.

The regular concert Tuesday evening of the Denver Symphony under Saul Caston was a program of music by Brahms and Rachmaninoff. William Kapell, sensational young pianist, was the featured soloist, and Laura Grauer, contralto, was soloist in Brahms' "Rhapsody." She was assisted by the male chorus of the Lamont Singers, Florence Lamont Hinman, director.

Kapell, a real favorite with the audience, went to town on the difficult pianisms of Rachmaninoff's "Third" piano concerto. This concerto is easily recognizable in light of its much more popular predecessor in this form. In some ways it is a better work but in perhaps more ways it is not. Sometimes it is of the same stuff as Beethoven, sometimes it is of Russian flavor, sometimes it is an amazingly sophisticated preview of the popular ballad style of the thirties in this country. From the standpoint of pure music there is an inconsistency and the over-all formal purpose is not clear, but whatever happens is fun while it is happening.

The soloist, playing very rhythmically, lightning fast when the occasion demanded, and with clean-cut clarity, combined with the orchestra to do an exciting reading of the concerto. With a particularly brilliant and well timed finish the audience was swept into an exceptionally spontaneous response. The lights were necessary to stop the applause, even after one encore at the end of the concert.

Miss Grauer, who has one of the best voices in town, did a fine peice of work in Brahms' subdued and introspective "Alto Rhapsody." There are some bare spots in the score which make singing a bit of a task for the soloist, and she was in control at all times. The male chorus carried out its assignment with a beautiful and well balanced tone.

The performance of Brahms' "Fourth Symphony" seemed in some places to have lost an edge which may have been worn off in the recent broadcast of this work by the orchestra. There were roughnesses of various minute kinds popping up now and then, and certain passages were cool. This, along with the fact that certain types of passages in the German romantic literature are not exactly down the alley for this orchestra, made the reading not entirely successful for this writer. A heavier and less brilliant orchestra color must be attained to project many of the spots in this work, and this color is not easy to get, nor is it really useful in any other styles of music. In addition to this was the feeling of sacrificing over-all line, especially the lovely slow movement, by too careful and predominant attention to individual measures, harmonies and other details, an approach which is so successful in French music, but which in this particular movement scherzo movement, on the other hand was of first rate order

---

MUSIC

By VIRGIL THOMSON

FEB. 26. 1947.

William Kapell

PHILADELPHIA ORCHESTRA, Eugene Ormandy, conductor, eighth New York concert of the season last night at Carnegie Hall. Soloist, William Kapell, pianist. The program: Variations on a Theme by Haydn......Brahms Symphony No. 2, Op. 35......Paul Creston Piano Concerto No. 3, in C major......Prokofieff Suite from "The Fire Bird"......Stravinsky

Mostly Modern

THE program was lively and the playing exquisite at last night's concert of the Philadelphia Orchestra under Eugene Ormandy in Carnegie Hall. The Brahms Variations on a Theme of Haydn are from 1870. The other works played are of our century; and one of them, at least, is of our time. Stravinsky's "Fire-Bird" suite is pre-World War I, from 1910. Prokofieff's Third Piano Concerto is from early in the fabulous twenties, 1921, to be exact. Paul Creston's Second Symphony, of 1945, is posterior to the second world war. Each of these works has, in addition to its intrinsic interest, a specific expressivity of its own epoch that set off last night that of the others in a most happy way.

Mr. Creston's symphony, to take them backwards, is a masterful work, mature, sure of itself, technically free and structurally well-sustained. Its expression, in spite of the technical freedom, is conventional in feeling; and its orchestral color, in spite of the sure-handed instrumentation, is dark and a bit lugubrious. Its dance-finale, a sort of speeded-up bolero, leans for emphasis on mechanization rather than on personalized emotion. The whole is competent, impressive, not very original. It is not a provocative work, but it has assurance, weight and abundance.

Prokofieff's Third Piano Concerto is our century's most successful work in that form. Stravinsky's is more original, but it is hard to take. Those of Rachmaninoff are more popular, but they lack intellectual distinction. Katchaturian's and Shostakovich's essays in the engre fall even lower in that respect. And hardly any of the others come off at all. This one is full of good material, and its expressive variety is immense. It juxtaposes tenderness, violence, irony and the enxpansion of pure energy in a most invigorating way;

Piano soloist last night with the Philadelphia Orchestra

and its musical ingenuity is inexhaustible.

William Kapell's performance of the piano part was powerful, beautiful and in every way striking. A certain maturity has appeared in this artist's work that is to its advantage. Last night he showed no febrile violence, only controlled emphasis. And he neither pound nor played false notes.. His rendering of this difficult and exacting work was that of a master pianist and a master musician. That of the Philadelphia Orchestra is this, as in the other works, was rich and bright in sound and wonderfully harmonius as to balance.

The orchestra and its conductor were, indeed, in fine form. They gave us, after and before, a lovely "Fire Bird" and a lilting piece of Brahms. But these works belong to history. Let us not strive too hard to pin down their temporal essence. As vehicles for fine orchestral playing they are tried and true. They did not fail the Philadelphians last night.

Music

KAPELL AT TOP AS PIANIST—AND ONLY 24

Oct. 1946

By RAYMOND MORIN

William Kapell, who gave a spectacular performance of Tschaikowsky's "Concerto in B-flat" at the 87th Worcester Festival, was particularly informative when I interviewed him regarding his views on piano playing and advice to ambitious young students.

Having reached the top rung of the pianistic ladder at the age of 24, the career of Kapell (who is known as Willy by his friends) has progressed with almost unprecedented rapidity. Extraordinary as it may seem, he did not have his first piano lesson until he was ten years old. You may wonder how he happened to start then.

"A little girl who frequently visited my home in New York," he said, "played little piano pieces that intrigued me, and finally I begged my parents to let me take piano lessons from her teacher. She was Dorothea La Follette, herself a pupil of Josef Lhevinnes."

Miss La Follette was one of two women from whom Willy received his entire piano training. The other was Olga Samaroff of the Juilliard School of Music, who also made two appearances at the Worcester Festival.

From Miss La Follette he received a rigid course of technical study. By the hour he practiced scales, arpeggios, octaves and the other fundamentals of technic. He strongly urges much technic, and incidentally is a great admirer of Horowitz, whose technic he considers comparable to none.

"Technic," Kapell insists, "is acquired by hard work alone, and that means hours upon hours of diligent practice."

All pianists do not agree on this point. Some believe that a minimum of basic technical practice is sufficient and that the remainder is to be found in the pieces themselves.

Nervousness

I asked Willy if he is nervous before and during a performance. His reply was the same as that of Horowitz when asked him the same question a few years ago.

"I think most artists suffer from nervousness. The farther you go in a career the greater the responsibility. It's like risking your reputation each time you play in public. I don't worry about forgetting the score, but am always concerned as to how it is going to go."

"Pierre Luboshutz is the only pianist I know who can rival Willy's sense of humor. He knows how to tell a story and is a good listener. In fact, with he and Luboshutz are brilliant raconteurs, and an evening with both would be something to remember."

Willy's father, a quiet and genial gentleman, was with him at Worcester, and if you don't think small possessions mean a great deal to an artist, you should have seen the admiration he showed for the Festival pin his father had just given him. The autograph seekers gave him plenty of opportunity to use it while he was here!

Large Repertory

One phase of Kapell's pianism that amazes me is the fact that during the 13 years that he has played the piano, he has acquired a prodigious repertory. Two seasons ago, he played Rachmaninoff's "Concerto in G minor" at the Worcester Festival. His first dates after leaving Worcester this time were in Chicago, where he played on successive nights the Prokofieff "Third Concerto" and Brahms' "Concerto in B-flat major." Add to these the Tschaikowsky concerto played the other night, as well as those by Khachaturian, Chopin, etc. And don't forget his many concert programs.

Most of this repertory was acquired during his study with Mme. Samaroff, in the course of about six seasons. Fortunately, he learns new works with astonishing rapidity and memorizes them as he learns them. Much of the repertory that he plays in his concerts today are compositions that he learned at the Juilliard and has been perfecting ever since.

KAPELL

NEW STAR OF THE KEYBOARD

Youthful William Kap[ell] Into Ranks of Mature [...]

By MARGARET HARFORD

Two seasons ago a slight, nervous boy with a heavy thatch of dark hair and a way of turning away from his audience and peering into the orchestra as if embarrassed to be the center of so much attention, played the flashy Khachaturian Piano Concerto with Alfred Wallenstein and the Los Angeles Philharmonic Orchestra.

Everyone said promise stuck out all over this talented youngster but that his destination, like the destination of all "promising" performers, was unknown.

Last night at Philharmonic Auditorium, William Kapell lifted himself out of the "gifted young artist" class with a magnificent performance of the Rachmaninoff Rhapsodie on a Theme of Paganini, serving notice to his admirers in this vicinity that he is a pianist with a capital P, and that all he needs is yet a little time to become a great one.

With all due respect to conductor and orchestra for what was an equally pleasurable program of Mozart's Symphony No. 39, Hindemith's symphonic synthesis of his opera "Mathis der Maler" and Three Cyprus Serenades by Anis Fuleihan, the evening belonged to young Kapell.

Kapell, now 25 but looking younger, left several indications [...]

Music

Kapell Exhibits Wizardry With Prokofieff Concerto

By LOUIS BIANCOLLI

One of the season's topflight readings occurred in Carnegie Hall last night when William Kapell ran off Prokofieff's Third Piano Concerto with Eugene Ormandy and the Philadelphia Orchestra.

Adding a note of drama to the stirring rendering was the tiny white finger bandage fluttering through the heaving bravura. Young Kapell was playing one of the world's toughest concertos with a badly cut finger!

On any count, last night's reading was this virtuoso's best showing to date. Giant technic romped through the hurtling rhythms like child's play, and tone and style fell into line.

Mr. Kapell's keyboard mastery seems to grow with every appearance — and he began with more than many pianists end with. As of last night I would say he sports one of the five best technics in the trade.

Hazardous Concerto.

The Prokofieff concerto is a whole mine-field of hazards. Spots in it would seem to call for several more than the regulation 10 fingers. A bruised finger-tip would ordinarily spell disaster.

The finger-twisting sequences crop up by the hundred here, and there are one or two passages the only parallel to which would be a Greeley Square traffic snarl.

But Mr. Kapell had it all moving smoothly. The heaping jumble of notes all glittered snugly into place, and the lad's two hands played leap-frog in breath-taking style.

Keen Idiomatic Flair.

Technic, gripping as it was to watch and hear, was still only the surface of last night's performance. Prokofieff, after all, isn't a mountebank; and neither is William Kapell.

The brash modernist mood, flashing with the tangy twists and turns of probing drama, came through the reading with keen idiomatic flair.

And Mr. Kapell seemed to sense the motive behind every melody, as if he had glimpsed Prokofieff's thought-processes in the making. It was all strictly in the groove.

You couldn't blame the crowd for bringing him out for repeated ovations — with the brilliance still ringing in everybody's ears.

Mr. Ormandy and the orchestra also rated high praise for the slick accompaniment applied. The teamwork was flawless, and the band played like one collective virtuoso.

Much the same standard held for the remainder of the program, which included Brahms' Variations on a Theme of Haydn's, Stravinsky's Fire Bird Suite, and Paul Creston's Second Symphony.

Creston Score Returns.

The Creston score returned after two years with augmented force. Earlier reservations seemed to vanish in the light of Mr. Ormandy's fresh exposition of its power.

Last night, this teeming web of Americana struck me as Creston's sturdiest score to date. Certainly the second movement ranks with the finest in recent symphonic striving.

Wagner called Beethoven's Seventh Symphony the "Apotheosis of the Dance." Mr. Creston went Beethoven one better by planning his as an "Apotheosis of Song and Dance."

I would reserve judgment about the song part of the plan; but anybody from Martha Graham to a galloping jitterbug would have found some handy dance rhythms in the symphony.

"His playing has depth and poetry and fire"—(Claudia Cassidy, Chicago Tribune)

HEAR William KAPELL

with the U. S. Steel Summer series of the
NBC SYMPHONY — Alfred Wallenstein, conducting,
Concerto No. 2 (1st movement)...Rachmaninoff
and piano solos
"Traumerei"...Schumann — "Gato"...Napolitano

SUN. EVE., JUNE 18 • 8:30 to 9:30 (EDST)
NBC NETWORK

Other Kapell summer engagements:
JUNE 22: Stadium Concerts with New York Philharmonic-Symphony,
JUNE 29: Robin Hood Dell, JULY 8, 11: Ravinia Festival with Chicago Orchestra

Management: JUDSON, O'NEILL & JUDD, Inc. • 113 West 57th Street, New York 19, N. Y.
RCA Victor Red Seal Records • Division of Colu...

THROUGH THE AGES TO NOW...
MASTERFUL MUSIC BY RCA VICTOR
ARTISTS. ALWAYS THE SAME HIGH
QUALITY...ALWAYS THE SAME LOW COST

William Kapell
exclusive RCA Victor
Recording Artist

As easy as placing a record on your "Victrola"*... as convenient as your record library shelf. Celebrated concert stars are naturally yours on RCA Victor Records for hours of listening pleasure. Your RCA Victor Dealer will be pleased to demonstrate any records from this fine selection of RCA Victor Recordings.

*"Victrola" T. M. Registered U. S. Pat. Off.
CONCERTO FOR PIANO AND ORCHESTRA No. 2, IN B-FLAT, Op. 19, Beethoven. William Kapell, Pianist, with the NBC Symphony Orchestra, Vladimir Golschmann, Cond. — Also included as Final Side in this Album: INTERMEZZO IN E, Op. 116, No. 6, Brahms. William Kapell, Pianist.
Album No. DM-1132................Four 12" Records................List Price $6.00

CONCERTO FOR PIANO AND ORCHESTRA (1936), Khatchaturian. William Kapell, Pianist, with the Boston Symphony Orchestra, Serge Koussevitzky, Conducting.
Album No. DM-1084................Four 12" Records................List Price $6.00

EVOCACION (from "Iberia Suite"), Albeniz. (Final Side in Album) MEFISTO WALTZ (Episode: The Dance in the Inn from Lenau's "Faust"), Liszt. William Kapell, Pianist.
Album No. DM-1101................Two 12" Records................List Price $3.50

PRELUDE IN C-SHARP MINOR, Op. 3, No. 2, Rachmaninoff. William Kapell, Piano.
12" Record No. 11-8824..$1.25

SONATA FOR VIOLA AND PIANO IN F MINOR, Op. 120, No. 1, Brahms. William P... and William Kapell, Pianist.
Album No. DM-1106................Three 12" Records................List Price $4.75

PRICES SHOWN ARE SUGGESTED LIST EXCLUSIVE OF TAX

LISTEN TO "MUSIC AMERICA LOVES BEST" ON THE RCA
VICTOR SHOW AT 4:30 P.M. EVERY SUNDAY OVER WMAQ

RCA VICTOR DISTRIBUTING CORP.
CHICAGO

Kapell used the media — particularly radio and recordings — to reach a much larger audience than would have been possible even thirty years earlier.

RADIO CORPORATION OF AMERICA
RCA VICTOR DIVISION
CAMDEN, NEW JERSEY

February 26, 1947

Miss Elizabeth Winston
Hope Associates
40 East 49th Street
New York 17, New York

Dear Miss Winston:

Everything went according to schedule on the William Kapell promotion over this past week-end and I feel that our efforts were well justified. In addition to making a terrific impression on Philadelphia Orchestra audiences, he was also quite cooperative within the limits of his very heavy week-end schedule.

We arranged an interview broadcast over WFIL Philadelphia, Friday night; this went very well in every respect. We got all-Kapell recorded programs on WPEN Philadelphia, Saturday night, including concert plugs, and again on Sunday over WFIL-FM, Philadelphia, Sunday night.

In addition, the Warwick Hotel, where he stopped, took pictures of him in the lobby for the Kirkeby Hotel magazine which is distributed each month to all Kirkeby Hotels throughout the United States, including New York, Philadelphia, Chicago, Beverly Hills and Havana. I shall send you copies when the picture appears.

Thank you again for your help in lining up this promotion, which produced a very favorable action in-so-far-as I was able to get reports. Hoping we can work together again some day soon, with kind regards,

Yours sincerely,

John Gruenberg, 2nd
Advertising Section
Record Department

lae

KAPELL PLA...
RODZINSKI...

William Kapell...
the New York Philharmon...
Sunday afternoon, Nov. ...
Fifth Symphony (E min...
mission speaker will...
of Rochester's Insti...
See?".

A biograph...
that he taught hims...
menian city of Tif...
impulsive statemen...
within range of a...
Khatchatourian, ...
the unmistakable...

His pi...
the work throu...
ian's acquaint...
principal orc...
Philadelphia ...
chance to he...
certo.

THIS IS C...

BUCKEYE BROADCASTING COMPANY **WSAI** *Kapell*
115 EAST FOURTH STREET
Cincinnati 2, Ohio

December 9, 1946

Miss Lorraine Lerner
The Earle Ferris Company
40 East 49th St.
New York 17, N. Y.

Dear Miss Lerner:

Thank you very much for your letter of November 26 in which you made William Kapell available to WSAI for an interview during his stay in Cincinnati.

Through the Women's Symphony Committee I understand that he has already been scheduled to take part in our weekly Symphony promotion program, "Symformation Quiz". On the same day, Thursday, December 12, we would be most happy to have him interviewed on "Time for Calling", 4:15-4:40 PM ... a program dedicated to the discussion of music and art and conducted by Miss Kay Hamilton. This would be convenient for Mr. Kapell in view of the fact that "Symformation Quiz" is recorded at 5:15 PM for delayed broadcast - same day - at 10:00 PM. He could make both appearances with but one visit to the studio.

I will contact Mr. Kapell on Wednesday at the Netherland Plaza but I would appreciate it if you would include the "Time for Calling" interview on his Cincinnati itinerary.

Sincerely,

Virginia Weber
Virginia Weber
Public Service Director

A *Marshall Field* STATION

MADISON AVENUE, NEW YORK 22, N.Y.

November 18, 1946

...URIAN CONCERTO;
...IKOWSKY'S FIFTH

...hatchatourian Piano Concerto with
...under Artur Rodzinski's direction
...00-4:30 PM, EST). Tschaikowsky's
...e balance of the program. The inter-
...O'Brien, director of the University
...cs. His topic is "How Much Can We

...hatchatourian makes the observation
... rhythms as a young child in the Ar-
...ing on a copper kettle. This may be an
...ing the proclivities of any young child
... kettle, but, in any case, the works of
...st, educated along traditional lines, bear
...e exotic folk-rhythms of Armenia.
..., for the most part a fiery piece, has been
...American audiences have made Khatchatour-
... has played it with most of the nation's
...teners to CBS' "Invitation to Music" and
...adcasts, however, have had the additional
...an composer's two symphonies and Violin Con-

* * *

COLUMBIA BROADCASTING SYSTEM

MEMORANDA

POOR PIANOS —
PITTSBURGH — TOO STIFF / DULL
KANSAS CITY — AWFUL
DENVER — TERRIBLE
PORTLAND — APPALLING
LONGVIEW, WASH. — EXCELLENT(!)
SEATTLE — BAD
VICTORIA — TOO DULL

1948 **JANUARY**
THURSDAY
New Year's Day — 1

At the Manhattan docks in 1947, preparing to board for a European tour. (Above) Wherever Kapell went, he kept a careful log of the pianos he played. (Right) His touring schedule was rigorous, as his 1947 diary reveals.

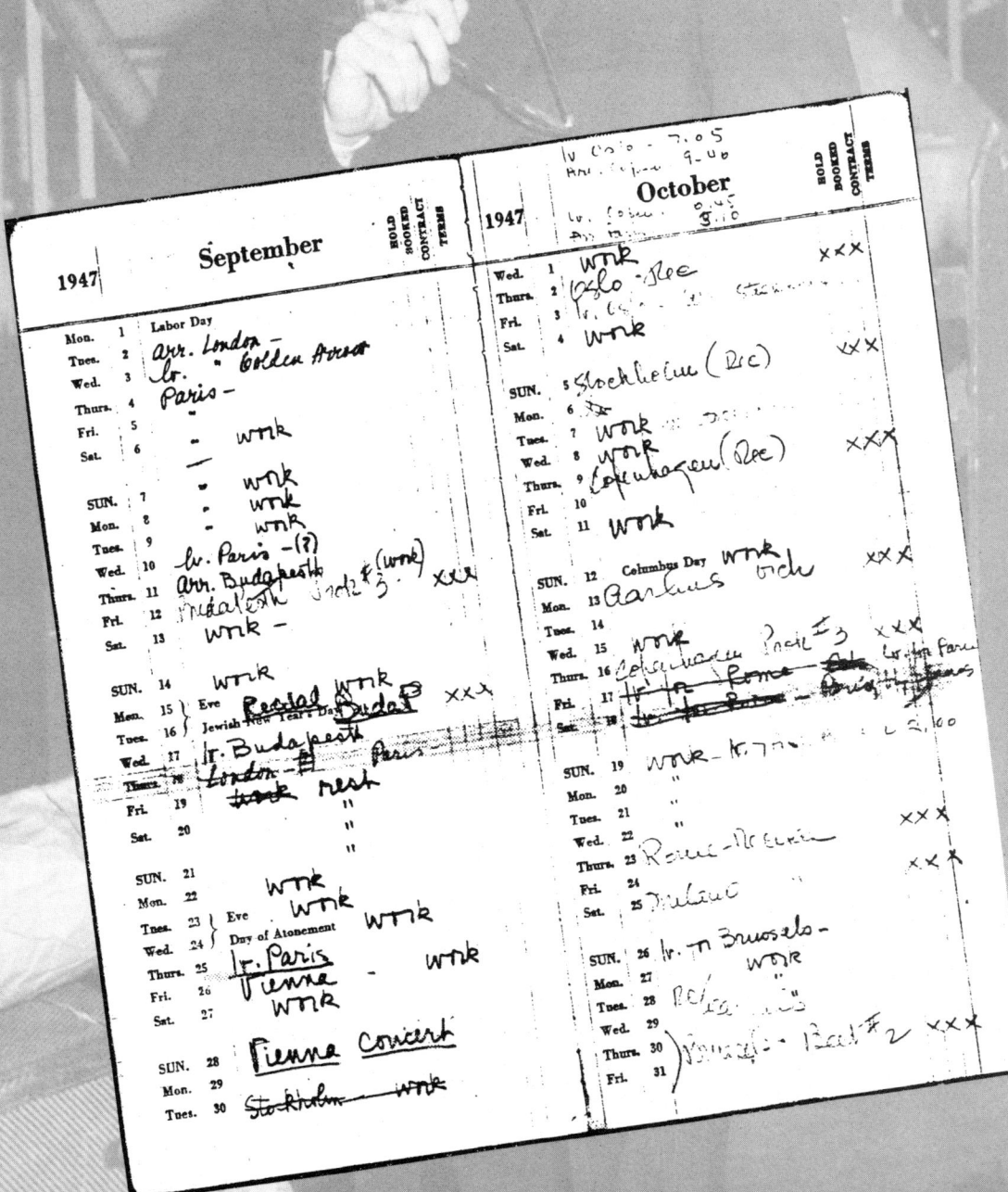

Rebecca Anna Lou Melson at the time of her marriage to William Kapell. (Above) Anna Lou takes a lesson from Sergei Tarnowsky, with whom she worked in Portland and Chicago; Tarnowsky also taught Vladimir Horowitz, Alexander Uninsky and Horacio Gutierrez.

Two rather somber photographs of the newlywed Kapells, taken immediately after their wedding.

In the summer after their wedding, the Kapells left for an extended tour of South America. (Right) The *NBC Bell Telephone Hour* was perhaps the most prestigious program of broadcast music in the United States; it lasted well into the television era. Anna Lou and Kapell are seen backstage before the broadcast.

MUSIC NEWS FROM

Kapell book
PR 34

Program for June 14

**WILLIAM KAPELL, YOUNG AMERICAN PIANIST, TO PLAY
RACHMANINOFF SELECTION IN FIRST
'TELEPHONE HOUR' APPEARANCE**

NEW YORK, June 4 -- William Kapell, young American pianist, will make his first appearance on NBC's "Telephone Hour" Monday, June 14 (NBC, 9:00 p.m., EDT).

Kapell has ... in this country ... in Europe and Australia as well as ... leave for a tour of ... rance on this program, he will

The pian... tra, under direction ... by the Bell Symphonic Orchestra, Rachmaninoff's "Conce... in the first movement of has become one of th... ter's works. Ke... recent ... work in B Minor" ... late Kapell's ...

Dance No. ...

... " by T...

AMERICA'S N...

(... ne 4, 1948)

...ADCASTIN...

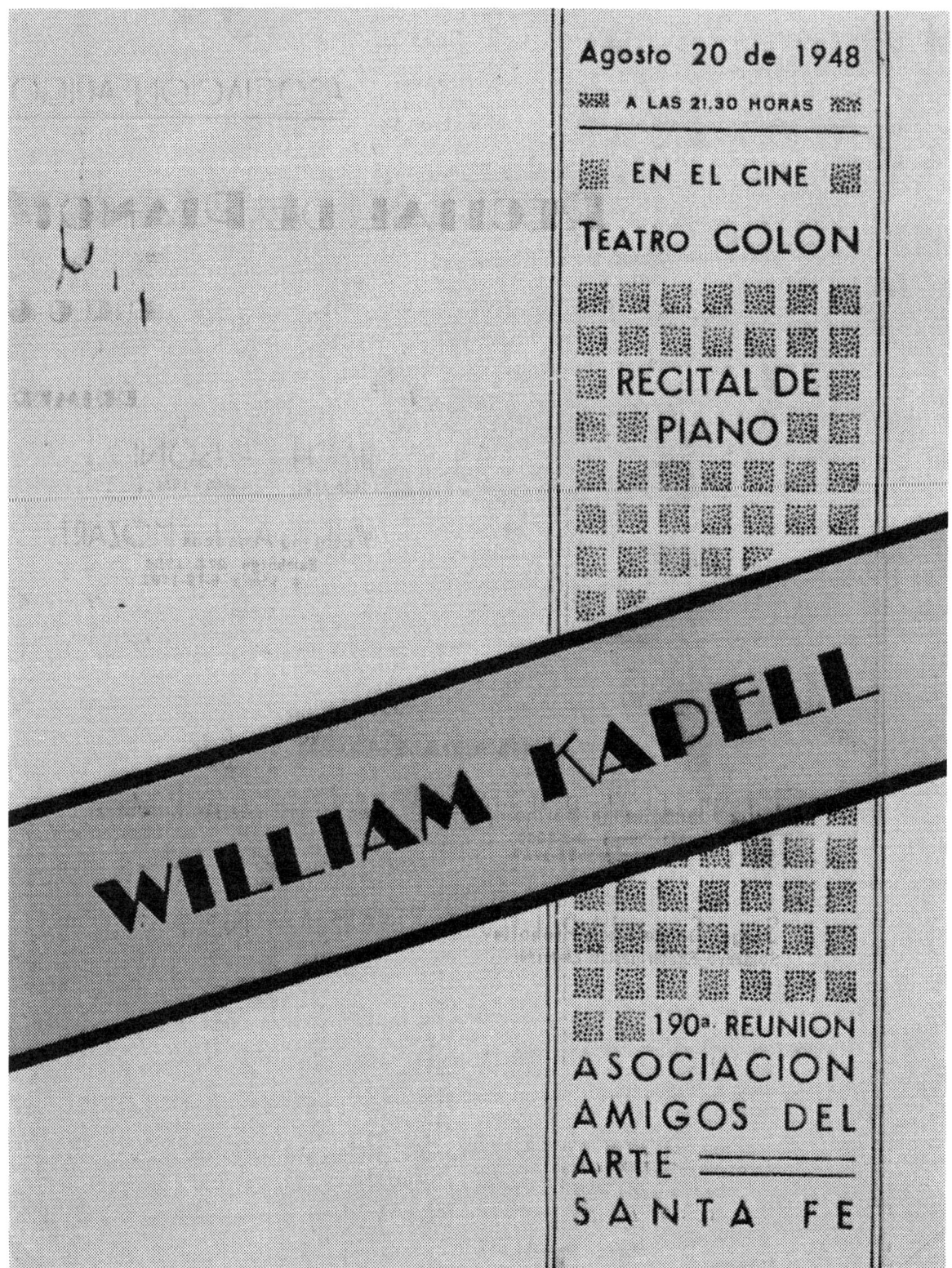

ASOCIACION AMIGOS DEL ARTE - SANTA FE

Recital de Piano: WILLIAM KAPELL

PROGRAMA

PRIMERA PARTE

BACH - BUSONI
1685-1750   1866-1924

Tres Corales - Preludios

Wolfgang Amadeus MOZART
Salzburgo 27-1-1756
† Viena 5-12-1791

SONATA en do mayor K. 330
  Allegro Moderato
  Andante cantabile
  Allegretto

SEGUNDA PARTE

Felix Mendelssohn Bartholdy
Hamburgo 3-2-1809
† Leipzig 4-11-1847

Tres Canciones sin Palabras

Sergei Sergeiwitch Prokofiev
Solnzevo-Ekaterinoslau 23-4-1891

SONATA N.º 7

TERCERA PARTE

Federico Francisco CHOPIN
Zelazowa - Wola 22-10-1810
† París 17-10-1849

Polonesa Fantasia
Mazurka en la bemol
Nocturno en si mayor
Scherzo en si menor

No se permitirá el ingreso a la sala durante la ejecución de los distintos números del programa —

A typical program from the 1948 South American tour, from a recital at Teatro Colon in Buenos Aires.

Some publicity material from the South American tour. (Above right) Anna Lou took this photograph of Kapell at a plaza in downtown Buenos Aires.

WILLIAM KAPELL

Kapell nació el 20 de Septiembre de 1922, de descendencia Española, Rusa y Polaca, y tal vez a eso se puede atribuir su afinidad con la música de los compositores Eslavos e Hispánicos. Willy - como lo llaman familiares y amigos - estudió primero con la señora Dorothea Anderson La Follete, mas tarde con Olga Samaroff Stokoswski, quien ha sido una de las grandes influencias musicales de su vida. Antes de cumplir los 20 años habia ganado tres premios importantes: el concurso juvenil de la orquesta de Filadelfia, el premio de la Fundación Naumburg y el premio de la beca de la Alcaldia.

Al celebrarse el 70.º cumpleaños del Dr. Koussevitzky, fué Kapell el que tuvo el honor de tocar en ese acontecimiento memorable.

TRANSLATION OF THE PRESS ON WILLIAM KAPELL

Het Dagblad, Nov. 13, 1947

William Kapell, a pianistic phenomenon: .... After this event of creative greatness the production of the young American pianist W.K. was an event of reproductive mastership. We don't have much admiration for the 3rd concerto for piano by Rachmaninoff. It lacks in its overloaded score the intimacy of the 2nd concerto. Besides it is for pianists a task of which only very few are capable. To those very few W.K. belongs, who rendered this work with an enormous élan and elementary musical passion. This pianist possesses unlimited technical possibilities to which one listens quite agasp.

De Waarheid, Nov. 13, 1947

The young American pianist W.K. presented [...] the 3rd concerto by Rachmaninoff, for [...] st job of the piano litterature [...]
Kapell - form[...] the heaps of notes. In [...] to be the executor of t[...] t keep him from omitting [...] s not important, for t[...] is entirely justifi[...]

De Maasbode, No[...]

...... Then W.K[...] triumph. He played the 3[...] ally brilliant and [...] e sultry romanticism of t[...] althy a way.
The soloist recei[...] self to Schuurman and the [...]

De Nieuwe Courant[...]

A young pianist fr[...] e 3rd concerto of Rachma[...] d. The enormous ovation c[...] s a flaming musicality [...] cer-tainly hear more of [...]

Haagsch Dagblad, Nov[...]

The second [...] American soloist, W.[...] concerto by Rachmanin[...] 3rd other themata and pom[...] e of by him with a passion [...] red us and put us out of c[...] ask for more rehearsals th[...] occur more serious deraillem[...] by Schuurman, whom Kapell ows part of his [...]

Algemeen Handelsblad, Nov. 13, 1947

After the intermission we got the surprise of the debute of the hardly 25 years old American pianist W.K. who played the 3rd Rachmaninoff concerto in a masterly fashion. This opus is only very seldom heard, but it us much more important than the well known second, it does not only require an enormous technical skill, but

---

ROYAL ALBERT HALL
(Manager—C. S. TAYLOR)

Sunday, November 16th, 1947, at 3 p.m.

The Orchestral Concerts Society Ltd.

present the

LONDON SYMPHONY ORCHESTRA
(Leader: GEORGE STRATTON)

SOLOIST:

WILLIAM KAPELL

CONDUCTOR:

SIR MALCOLM SARGENT

Management ... HAROLD HOLT LTD.

it is much more important than the well known second; it does not only require an enormous technical skill, but also temperament, a capacity for moulding and romantic pathos.
Kapell proved to be a pianist of outstanding quality. His powerful forto is always ... besides he conjures the finest shades in transparant ligh... of his technic is wonderfully skillfil, in ... towering passion and a rich musicality. ...
course an ovation- ...
man take part, who ... is
"obsessed" soloist ...

NORSK KONSERTDIREKSJON

William Kapell

Eneste konsert

Torsdag 2nen oktober 1947 kl. 20
Universitetets Aula

★

PROGRAM

I

Bach-Liszt: Fantasi og fuge g-moll

Mozart: Sonate, C-dur, K. 330
Allegro moderato
Andante cantabile
Allegretto

II

Chopin: Sonate, op. 58, b-moll
Allegro maestoso
Scherzo molto vivace
Largo
Finale. Presto non tanto

Pause

III

Mendelssohn: 3 sanger uten ord

Prokofieff: Sonate, nr. 7
Allegro inquieto
Andante caloroso
Precipitato

★

Konsertflygel fra Grøndahl A.s

Het Binnenhof, Nov...

...... After the ... st,
25 years old, fro...
of The Hague and ...
piano concerto by ... ,
he plays also th...
flutists, every ...
And he also capt... st
who is going to ...

Trouw, Nov. 13, ...

.... It is a pi... nly
manifested itse... rto
by Rachmaninoff ... the
25 years old A... in
comparison wit... ering
technical skil... ty. In
the first and ... of the
orchestra, wh... ompact
heaps of note... 2nd
concerto, how... ach-
maninoff's u... by this
the impopula... ous
requirements ... wever,
conquered al... ormous
technical c...

Nieuwe Haag...

The 25 year... and beautifully ins... in a rendition tha... es not only possess a ... usical intuition. ... thos. The orchestra... ul.

Haagsche Courant, ...

The 25 years old American piani... e climax of the evening with Rachmaninoff's 3rd concer... 30 which is only little played since being madly difficult. K. proved to be entirely worth of the fame that preceded him.
He is a phenomenal instrumentalist and a highly gifted artist with a security and elegance of playing, in comparison to which c... cities not only the Residentie Orchestra would be distanced
do hpe to see Kapell back very soon!

Mr. and Mrs. William Kapell with their son David, photographed in 1949 in La Jolla, California.

Still in his mid-20s, Kapell was celebrated by audiences and critics. In the years remaining to him, Kapell would both steady and deepen his art, and the result, as captured in his late recordings, was a unique blend of passion and repose.

Part Three : Mastery

*T*he last five years of Kapell's life were his most fulfilling. The tours, recordings, and practice sessions continued at an exhausting pace. Yet during this time, he grew to maturity as an interpreter, turning from the flashy Russian showpieces that had made him famous and focusing increasingly on the music of Bach, Mozart, Beethoven, Schubert and Chopin. With Anna Lou, he built a successful marriage, and he delighted in his children, David Eugene Melson Kapell, born May 4, 1949 in Los Angeles, and Rebecca Ellen Kapell, born April 30, 1951 in New York.

"He considered himself a good father," Anna Lou recalls, "and we were generally very happy together. We made the effort to travel as a family when he was playing in the United States. There were difficult times, of course. Being a successful performer — particularly such a self-critical performer — can make for a stressful life. And he had inherited one aspect of his temperament from his mother, a certain anxiety that expressed itself in physical agitation. At my urging, he finally consulted a therapist, who helped him quite a bit. You can hear it in the recordings."

"He was a person of extremes," she continued. "On the one hand, he was terribly insecure, particularly when he was younger, and it bothered him deeply that he was already considered a great artist with an important career, for which he many times felt that he was inadequately prepared. But he also always knew, deep down, that he was very gifted. He knew that he could just walk onto the stage and have the audience eating out of his hand. That was an experience he knew from a very young age. His presence was indeed very powerful and very electric. He caught audiences up with the power of his concentration, his songfulness and the inexorable strength of his rhythmic sense — like Serkin, like Horowitz."

In the early 1950s, two of the world's most celebrated pianists were living on the same block in Manhattan. Vladimir Horowitz occupied the townhouse at 14 East 94th Street (where he died in 1989) while the Kapells lived on the first two floors of 21 East 94th Street, across the street and slightly to the east. The two pianists, while never close friends, saw one another fairly regularly, and Anna Lou remembers particularly an evening when they visited Horowitz at his home and the two men played for one another until after midnight.

Samaroff had died in 1948 (ironically, on the Kapells' wedding day) and Kapell had participated in a memorial concert in her honor. Shortly thereafter, he began to teach. At the time of his death, he was to have joined the faculty at The Juilliard School (his close friend, the pianist Laura Fratti, was to work regularly with his students while he was on tour). His first student was Jerome Lowenthal, who studied with him at the request of Fredric Mann, and has left a vivid memory of their association:

> Twenty-seven years old and a figure of gauche dynamism, over whose face the sweetest of smiles and the angriest of frowns played in unpredictable alternation, Kapell seemed like the very flame of art. His playing was quite simply electrifying, and for several years I had sought out opportunities to hear him play. Like me, he had been a Samaroff student; like me, he had been helped by Fredric Mann. I was at the age when the First Commandment seems unimportant and it is hardly surprising that, even before I had met him, Kapell had become my god.

After extracting a promise from Lowenthal that he would henceforth practice "at least" five hours a day, Kapell accepted him as a pupil. "The form of the lessons was variable," Lowenthal recalled. "Sometimes he would begin by asking what I had been thinking about music, and if, in my answer, I chanced to stumble on a phrase that interested him, he might improvise variations upon it until I felt like Diabelli contemplating the erection of Beethoven's cathedral on the scaffolding of his little waltz. At first we worked a lot on finger-strengthening, using scales and arpeggios, Czerny and the right hand of the Chopin B minor Scherzo. Later, he continued to talk about the importance of having steel in the fingers but left me to my own devices as to how to acquire it."

"The one thing that was consistent about the lessons was the intensity of Kapell's commitment and the generosity of his spirit. When he was pleased with my playing, a holiday was declared: his wife, the beautiful Anna Lou, was called in, and my heart sang. If he was displeased, he showed it dryly and directly: 'That wasn't good a-t-all!' and my hands swam in sweat. The awe that I felt for him was, in truth, not unmixed with fear, but I never doubted the strength of his commitment to our work together."

Harold C. Schonberg, newly arrived at the *New York Times* (where he would eventually ascend to the position of chief music critic from 1960 to 1980), wrote a perceptive review of a March 1951 recital, which deserves quotation at some length:

> For the last few years one has been wondering if William Kapell was going to be a permanent member of the 'promising' group of younger pianists. Of his innate talent, there never was any doubt. The question concerned the direction in which he was headed: sterility and mannerism versus musicianship and imagination. His concert last night in Town Hall did much to resolve the issue.

> It showed that Mr. Kapell is on his way to becoming one of the great pianists. It showed a clarification of the emotional problems that must have beset him, and it showed a maturity far in advance of anything he has displayed in this city.
>
> This maturity was reflected in his program. Artistry involves a knowledge of what not to play even more than a knowledge of what to play. Too many young pianists rush to program music with which they have no emotional affinity. In the past Mr. Kapell has been guilty of this offense. Last night, though, he confined his attention to four pieces — Bach's D major Partita, the Copland Sonata, Debussy's 'Children's Corner' and Liszt's Eleventh Rhapsody.
>
> These pieces he understood. They were polished, they had proportion and finesse, and they were possessed of musical understanding. In addition, they sang out — and a singing tone in the past has been a rare experience at a Kapell recital.
>
> Of this pianist's perfect mechanism, no more need be said than that nothing bothers him, from the contrapuntal lines of Bach, to the awkward skips of Copland.

Kapell had always been interested in American music, but toward the end of his life he determined to become its champion. He almost always included either Copland's Variations or his Piano Sonata on his international tours. (The composer planned to write a lengthy work for him; the result, first played some four years after Kapell's death by William Masselos, was the Piano Fantasy, Copland's grandest and most ambitious piece for the instrument.) He told RCA Victor that he wanted to record works by Copland and Thomson, and he hoped to commission pieces from Vincent Persichetti, Ned Rorem, Norman Dello Joio and Peter Mennin, among others. In a letter to Thomson written in 1952 (now in the Thomson collection at Yale University) he outlined some of his thoughts about a program devoted entirely to American music planned for the 1953-54 season.

"As it is shaping up in my mind at present, I will play works by yourself, Sessions, Copland, Ives and possibly Ruggles," he wrote. "Too, there will be represented a member of my generation; who it shall be I don't know yet. I shall go through quite a bit of music before making a decision on that point.

"It seems to me a crying shame that some of the fine pieces in our native literature are not played more often," Kapell continued. "If we allow the present and lamentable accent on commerce and sensationalism to combine, our whole musical culture will be threatened. The situation today appears very serious and no little bit tragic. The powers that control this noble profession are making nitwits out of the large public. A public not interested in active participation at a concert, but a dull, complacent and uncultivated mass of grey. I, for one, am sick and tired of going along in any way with the public 'taste.' Many artists do not realize that by doing so they slowly are dying, creatively; and when artists die, so does art."

Kapell continued to record. Some Chopin discs — roughly half of the Mazurkas and the B minor Sonata (Op. 58) — are among the finest souvenirs of his later artistry, combining as they do the songfulness of Rubinstein with (when appropriate) the urgent forward motion of Horowitz and Kapell's own profoundly rooted sense of musical structure. A partial recording of the Bach Partita No. 4, left incomplete at Kapell's death and issued as part of a memorial album, is fascinating; with its contrapuntal clarity, lean, tensile sense of continuity and ecstatically personal understanding of the music, Kapell's performance, to a startling degree, prefigures the work of Glenn Gould.

A new friend was Jascha Heifetz, with whom Kapell planned to make recordings of the three violin sonatas by Johannes Brahms. Only the last of these, in D minor, ever came to fruition, but Kapell and the famously difficult violinist got along very well and, in addition to the Brahms sonatas, they spoke of recording the great trio literature with the cellist Gregor Piatigorsky. In June 1952, Heifetz came to dinner. "Divine evening, divine man, divine artist," Kapell wrote in his diary. "We played word games and talked, and Kufflet [a nickname for Anna Lou], Laura [Fratti] and I were absolutely unconscious all of the time. When 'he' left, no one dared sit in the chair 'he' had used."

("Heifetz loved Willy," Jack Pfeiffer, whose career as a producer and executive at RCA Victor, spanned more than 40 years, recalled in 1990. "He never forgave him for dying young.")

The last year of Kapell's life was devoted to a flurry of performances and concert tours. He visited Israel in May 1953, where he was delighted with the enthusiasm and sophistication of the audiences. Then he joined his family in Prades, a mountain village in France where Casals had established a summer music festival. There he performed Schubert lieder with Maria Stader, a Beethoven violin sonata with Arthur Grumiaux, and a Mozart concerto (K. 414) under the direction of Casals himself. Some private recordings exist from the Prades Festival, and they reflect the continuing evolution in Kapell's playing, in part inspired by his close friendship with Istomin and his exposure to Casals. "Casals as a man is one thing," he wrote to his friend, the pianist Shirley Rhoads. "And rather disappointing. But his way with Bach is something to adore. It has heart and soul. It is human and overflowing, and grand. It warms and soothes and makes happy. Isn't that what we all want?"

At the conclusion of the Prades Festival, Kapell and his family returned to the United States. Almost immediately, he left for an extended tour of Australia, arriving in Sydney on July 11, 1953. Over the course of the next 14 weeks he played 37 concerts, not just in Sydney and Melbourne but all over the continent — in places with names like Bendigo, Shepparton, Albury, Horsham and Goolong.

After the joys of the Prades Festival and the sophisticated audiences to which he had become accustomed in Europe and in Israel, Australia proved disheartening. Separated from his children (and, half the time, from Anna Lou as well), lonely and under constant stress, he found the Australians "a very basically unfriendly people, who should be left alone with their sullen thoughts of inferiority to the rest of the world. Maybe then they'd do something about raising their own standards."

Still, he played magnificently for them. It is impossible to listen unmoved to a broadcast tape of Kapell's final concert, with its tragic, tolling and ferociously dramatic reading of Chopin's "Funeral March" Sonata in B-flat (Op. 35). A tape of the performance circulated among collectors for years; when RCA Victor released it for the first time in 1987, the *New York Times* promptly selected it as one of the finest recordings of the year — this despite poor sound quality and, in fact, the less-than-optimum piano on which Kapell played.

On October 28, Kapell left at last for the United States. He had found his stay dispiriting and said as much to Eunice Gardner, of the Sydney *Daily Telegraph*, one of the few friends he had made in the Australian press. He blasted "Madhatter" critics and vowed that he would never return. And then he boarded a British Commonwealth Pacific Airline DC-6 that would carry him to Fiji, Canton Island, Honolulu and, ultimately, to San Francisco.

In the first edition of his book *Music To My Eyes*, Alfred Bendiner drew a caricature of Kapell, calling him "another jumpy pianist who won't relax and let it come to you." "He dashes on stage, plays like a marionette pianist — jerks his mane up and down as if his head was on a wire — and dashes off," Bendiner continued. Yet Kapell's late performances were characterized by serenity and songfulness, better captured in this meditative photograph from the early 1950s.

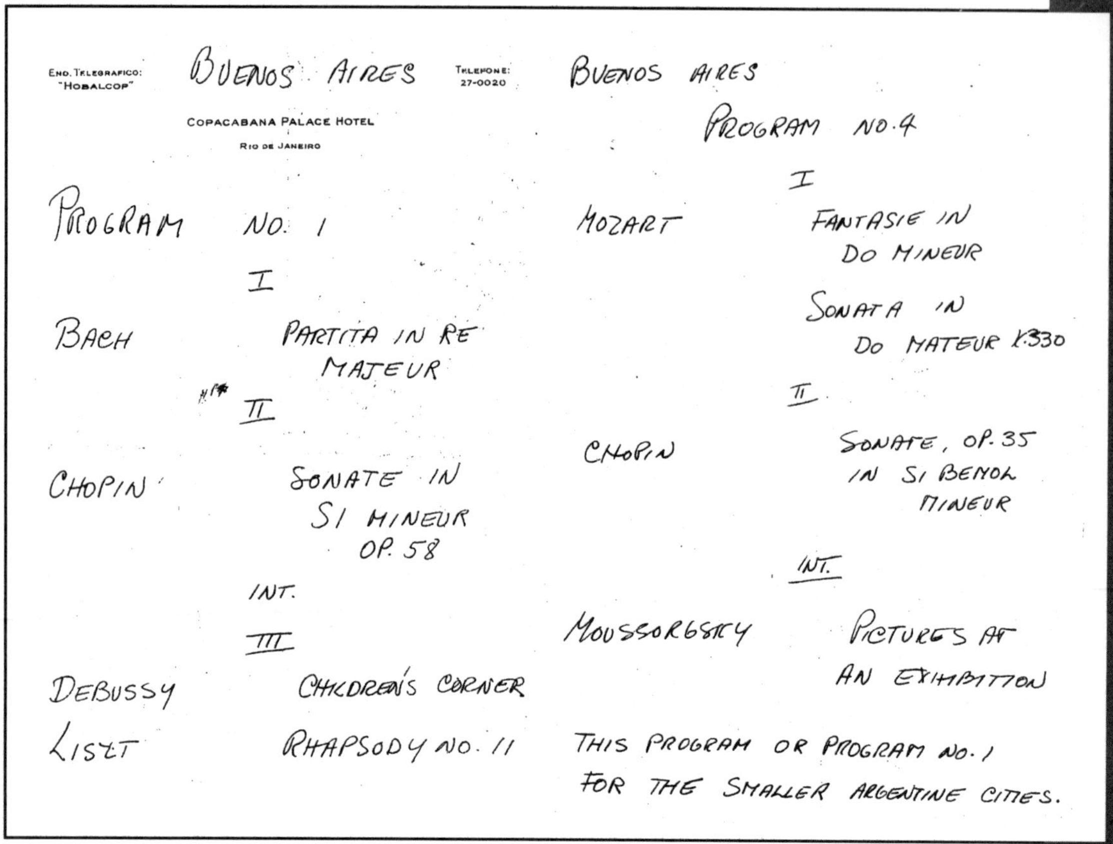

END. TELEGRAFICO: "HOBALCOP" TELEFONE: 27-0020

BUENOS AIRES

COPACABANA PALACE HOTEL
RIO DE JANEIRO

BUENOS AIRES

PROGRAM NO. 1

I

BACH — PARTITA IN RE MAJEUR

II

CHOPIN — SONATE IN SI MINEUR OP. 58

INT.

III

DEBUSSY — CHILDREN'S CORNER
LISZT — RHAPSODY NO. 11

PROGRAM NO. 4

I

MOZART — FANTASIE IN DO MINEUR
SONATA IN DO MAJEUR K. 330

II

CHOPIN — SONATE, OP. 35 IN SI BEMOL MINEUR

INT.

MOUSSORGSKY — PICTURES AT AN EXHIBITION

THIS PROGRAM OR PROGRAM NO. 1 FOR THE SMALLER ARGENTINE CITIES.

With Kapell's increased maturity as man and artist came a dedication to the masterpieces of the piano repertory, as these drafts for some Latin American concerts in 1951 attest.

```
BUENOS AIRES                              BUENOS AIRES
    PROGRAM NO. 2                              PROGRAM NO. 3
            I                                          I
BACH-LISZT      PRELUDE AND            BACH        PARTITA, SI MINEUR
                FUGUE, LA MINEUR                   (NACH FRANZÖSISCHER
MOZART          SONATE, K.570                      ART)
                SI BEMOL
                                                       II
            II                         PROKOFIEFF      SONATE NO. 7
COPLAND         SONATA
                (1941)                     INT.

    INT.                                       III

            III                        DEBUSSY         SUITE BERGAMASQUE
SCHUMANN        KINDERSCENEN           DE FALLA    { ARAGONESA
CHOPIN          SCHERZO                              CUBANA
                SI MINEUR                            DANSE DU MEUNIER
```

Technique and Musicianship

By WILLIAM KAPELL

The goal of piano study is not finger dexterity as an end in itself, but as a means of releasing musical thought, says this brilliant young pianist

There seems to be a tendency among our generation of pianists to overvalue contemporary technical standards.

We often hear that technique stands at a higher level today than it did 40 years ago. This is perhaps true, in the sense that the general average of playing, by students as well as professionals, is higher than it used to be. Fingers are fleeter than formerly.

On the other hand, we can boast fewer pianistic giants. In the period ending around 1917, at least 18 towering pianists were performing—figures like Busoni, Paderewski, Rosenthal, Hofmann, Gabrilowitsch, Bauer to name but a few. Today, there are hardly ten who approach that stature.

It is significant that among those giants, technique as such was not the standard of phenomenal playing. The great ones stood out because of what they had to say.

Although I do not believe in futile enshrinings of the past, those earlier standards made it plain that the goal of piano playing is not finger development, but the release of musical thought through finger development. The pianist must have something of musical value to express in addition to the technical means for expressing it. And he reaches his happiest development when technique and musicianship maintain parallel progress.

To start with the technical aspects: It is helpful to begin study by believing that mere mechanics need not be dull. Too many students work on the theory that finger development is a kind of barbed-wire area of dismay where they are imprisoned until the happy moment when they can show a certain grade of fluency, only then being released to play music. Hence they play their finger-drills with the fingers alone, letting mind and spirit lose themselves in fanciful daydreams about the music to come. Such an attitude is harmful and mistaken. You can't separate technique from music.

What you can do is make technical work as musical as possible. There is beauty in the sheer skill of playing an even scale. One can derive pleasure from a rippling arpeggio, a warm, pearly touch, an absolute equality of the fingers.

Of course some pianists are born with a natural aptitude for mechanics. They are endowed by nature with better-than-average fingers, just as star athletes are endowed with superior reflexes. But sometimes it happens that those with the best natural technique work less than the others, and in the end find themselves eclipsed by the harder workers. Gifted hands as well as ungifted must be developed to fulfill their promise.

To make mechanics interesting, we must clarify their aim, not only as preparation for a Beethoven sonata, but at the moment of playing scales and exercises themselves. All tones of the daily exercises must be beautiful. Listen for beauty of tone while you play them slowly, quickly, legato, staccato, and at various dynamic levels.

For keyboard problems I know nothing better than the studies of Hanon. I was put on Hanon as a child, I still work at Hanon, and I have yet to find a finger difficulty for which Hanon does not provide a solution. In practicing for evenness of tone in Debussy's "Gradus ad Parnassum," I went back to the first study of Hanon. I have never had to devise special exercises. Scales, arpeggios and Hanon, practiced daily over the years, make one's fingers ready for any mechanical demands.

To get the most out of Hanon, one must play it as *music*. One must strive for control of touch and dynamics as conscientiously as in works for public performance. If you play Hanon mechanically, you are apt to play mechanically when you come to Chopin.

Another trick is to work for real finger independence, as if your fingers had no connections with wrists, arms, shoulders or back. While body weight is useful for legato singing tone, it is harmful to development of the complete finger-evenness required in Bach, Mozart and Scarlatti.

Make sure of passing the thumb with no twisting of the hand. If the hand jerks, bumps, unevenness, even wrong notes will result. This is true of arpeggios as well as of runs. The most difficult arpeggios, those of the dominant and diminished seventh in which the thumb goes under the fifth finger, need special attention to passing the thumb without hand motion.

But the best fingers in the world won't help you if you have no musical meaning for them to release. The development of musicianship is the responsibility of the teacher—preferably the first teacher, who shapes thought-patterns at their most impressionable stage.

The teacher should call attention to the need for beauty of tone and phrasing; the demands of style in music of various epochs; the interrelation of various techniques and touches. Youngsters must be shown why one doesn't play Mozart like Chopin—not when a recital is imminent, but from the beginning, at the first encounter with "pieces." They should be taught that Beethoven requires a different technique from Scarlatti because Beethoven enlarged the scope of keyboard playing.

I think of creative piano teachers as being like my own great teacher, Olga Samaroff. She was the greatest musical influence of my life. Lessons with her were like performances. She never played for her students, yet the imagination she put into each lesson made it vivid as the finest demonstration from the concert platform.

"Madame," as we called her, began by insisting on strictest attention to note-values, rests, and all other indications by the composer. In the first two lessons she made it clear that she would tolerate no carelessness in this respect. The student who did not comply was not allowed to come back.

Then came interpretative suggestions, never as blueprints for performance but as aids in stimulating the student's own imagination. To get sonority in a Bach organ fugue, she would ask you to imagine yourself hearing the work in a great cathedral, full of echoes, hollows, and reverberations of tones. Then she would ask you to try to duplicate such a tone on the piano. When she wanted rich, full tone in a passage, she would write "red-blooded" into the score.

Madame rarely explained technical details and muscular motions. She relied on imagery and suggestion to get the desired results. While she realized that many teachers explain muscular movements, and that many students need such instruction, she felt it to be harmful in the development of independent musical thought. Her belief was that if, over a period of time, the student could not intuitively sense the meaning of the music, it would do him small good to try for synthetic effects by holding his hands in a certain way.

When pupils over a long period showed no imagination and no receptivity, she would encourage them to give up trying for an artist's career and try other avenues of musical activity.

Among more than 200 lessons with Madame, the one that stands out in my memory dealt with the slow movement of Chopin's B Minor Sonata. For three hours she simply explained what this music meant to her. At the end of that time I had entered a new world, perceiving values I had never seen before—not only in the Chopin sonata but in the whole art of interpretation.

Taking the sonata bar by bar, she pointed out that to her the lyrical quality of the work, more grave than that found in the Nocturnes, reflects deep religious feeling. The mood is set by the rhythmic bass, above which the melody sings. She showed me that the middle section in E Major, often made tedious by rippling, superficial playing, is like a dream—all piano, not a forte in the entire passage—contrasting with the well-ordered formal pattern of the theme, and returning, at last, on a long progression in diminished sevenths, to a lyric restatement of the lyric opening, softened this time, but with the unmistakable suggestion of a march.

After elaborating her views in terms of an idea, a philosophy, a color or a picture, Madame would encourage the pupil to go on from there in his own way. Often she would begin a lesson away from the piano, asking me what I'd been thinking about. Never did she tell me *how* to play. If I couldn't dig that out of myself, so much the worse for me!

An idea of Madame's might come to life long after she had planted it—sometimes with unexpected results! That memorable lesson on the Chopin B Minor Sonata went churning around inside me, and soon after, I disregarded a Beethoven assignment and learned all the Chopin Mazurkas. At first Madame was furiously angry with me; but after I had explained my defection, she relented and was pleased.

That, to my mind, is truly great teaching. A student lucky enough to benefit from it approaches the piano with wider horizons. He knows that, besides training his fingers to be fleet, he must release musical values of his own. Then he begins to make music! THE END

Kapell summed up some of his ideas on musical training in this article for *Etude* Magazine, published in December 1950.

Kapell, shown here with conductor Pierre Monteux, rarely wore glasses, and photographs such as these are scarce. (Right) With Alexander "Sascha" Greiner, the long-time director of artists relations for Steinway and Sons.

Vladimir Horowitz insisted on sending his own piano to any city where he performed. Kapell did not quite go that far, but he kept careful track of the instruments he would consent to play on tour and, in later years, he would send a favorite Steinway to any engagements where he did not know the piano.

```
                    WILLIAM KAPELL
                    TOUR 1950/51

         CD 382
    ✓Dallas, Tex. - Jan. 9th
    ✓Ft. Worth, Tex. - Jan 10th                CD 81
    ✓New York City - Feb. 15, 16,
                              17 &18    ✓Chicago, Ill - Jan. 16th
    ✓Kansas City - Feb. 27th
    ✓Topeka, Kans. - March 2nd                 CD 362
    ✓Chicago, Ill. - March 8th
    ✓Pittsburgh, Pa. - Mar. 16th & 18th    ✓Corvallis - Jan. 22nd
     Philadelphia, - April 6th & 7th      ✓Berkeley - Jan. 26th
     Washington,D.C. - April 9th          ✓Alameda - Jan. 28th
     New York City - April 17th           ✓San Francisco - Jan. 30th
    ? Ann Arbor, Mich.- May 6th           ✓Los Angeles - Feb. 1st.
                                          ✓Fullerton - Feb. 4th
                                          ✓Long Beach - Feb. 5th
                                          ✓San Diego - Feb. 8th
                                          ✓Nashville - Feb. 20th
                                          ✓New York City - March 28th
                                           Urbana, Ill. - April 4th

                    LOCAL PIANOS
              San Francisco - Jan. 19th
              Spokane, Wash. - Jan. 24th
              Denver, Colo. - March 6th
              Granville - March 14th
              Lexington - March 20th
              Logan - April 12th
              Toronto - April 23rd
              Lincoln - May 1st
              Salt Lake City - May 15th
```

June — 1,500.00
500.00
July — 5,000

2829

Jascha Heifetz greatly admired Kapell and planned to play and record the three Brahms violin sonatas with him; only the third of these, in D minor (Op. 108) was ever recorded — a precious souvenir of what might have been a thrilling artistic partnership.

Steinway and Sons distributed handsome signed promotional photographs such as this one to leading music stores throughout the world.

Kapell Cites Parents' View On Careers

"The average American parent wants his child to enter the business world or one of the professions such as law or medicine —and is a little embarrassed if the child wants to be a musician."

KAPELL.

That was the opinion expressed here Friday by William Kapell, widely - known 30-year-old pianist. Kapell will play a concert for members of the Des Moines Civic Music association at 8:15 o'clock tonight at KRNT theater.

"A child who wants to be a musician is regarded by adults and his friends as kind of a sissy," Kapell said.

Cites Europe.

"Music in this country still is thought of as entertainment, rather than a necessary part of daily life," he said. "In Europe, music is indispensable. The people need it like food. Parents are proud if their child wants to study music."

He predicted, however, that in time music will gain the peak here that it has in Europe.

"In the last 10 years, there has been a tremendous growth of interest in music in the United States," he said.

Communities.

"More and more communities are sponsoring concerts, more

IN OLGA SAMAROFF MEMORIAL CONCERT

William Kapell, pianist, and the Juilliard String Quartet will be heard at Town H

Glimpses of a busy life: a formal tribute to "Madam;" a decidedly informal late-night session at the piano; a memento of a family vacation.

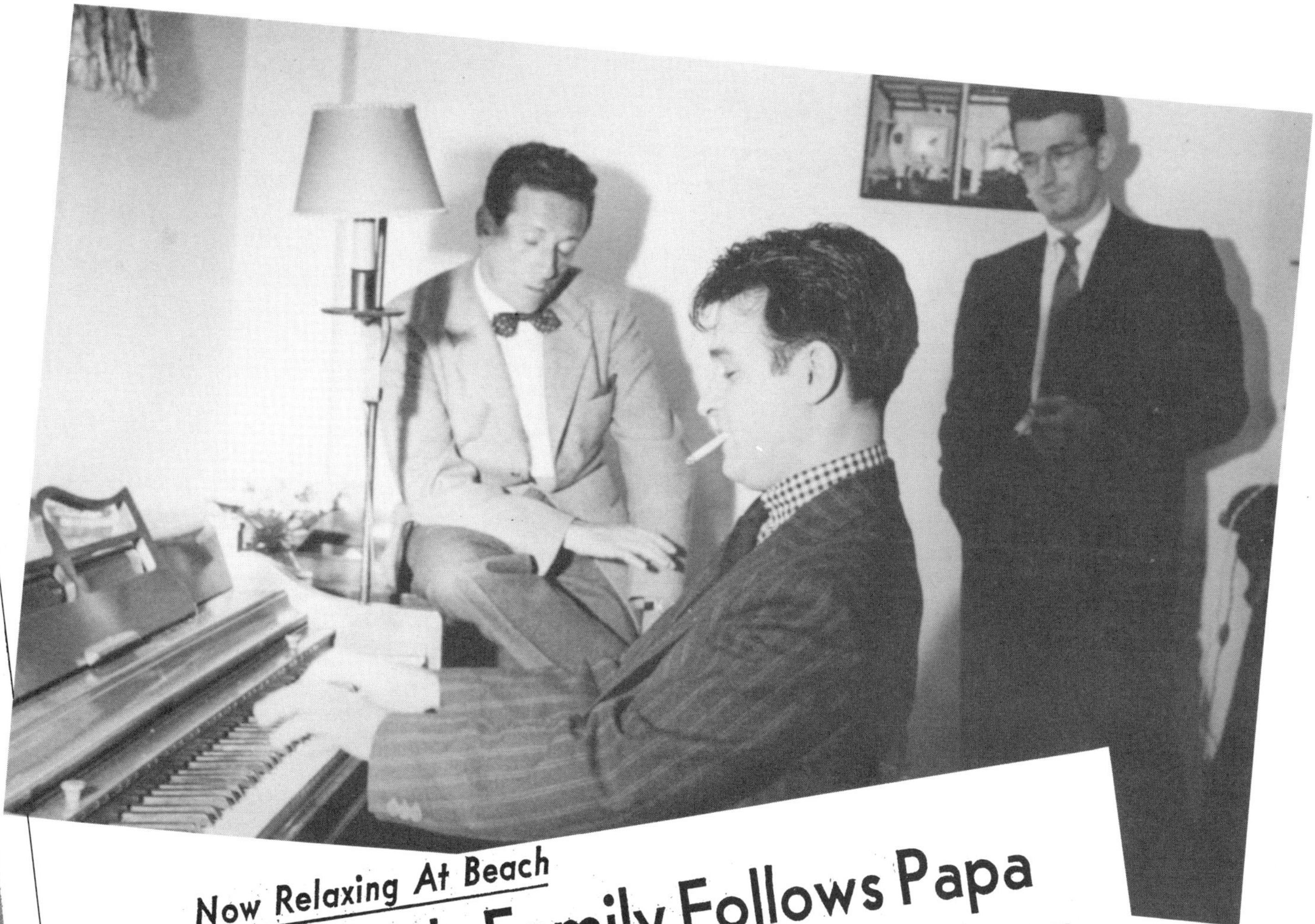

Now Relaxing At Beach
Pianist's Family Follows Papa

PASS-A-GRILLE BEACH — The wife of a concert pianist also finds life a whirlwind tour, since she and the children try for the most part to keep in step with the musician.

The pianist is William Kapell, 30-year-old virtuoso who is currently appearing with the leading orchestras and giving concerts in major cities the world over. Next Sunday he is to be featured with the New York Philharmonic.

His wife, Rebecca, and children, Becky and David, are now beaching for a week with the musician's parents, the Harry Kapells of Pass-a-Grille.

DAVID

The Kapells' life is virtually a constant race for the next plane. The family will meet in New York, home base, and start off again soon.

Two Years' Roaming

"We're packing furniture and becoming vagabonds until 1955," Mrs. Kapell said. "It'll be a good two years before we settle."

The itinerary includes France, Prades in the Pyrenees, the Pablo Casals festival, Israel and Australia for three and one-half months.

After the Australia tour sans children, the Kapells are to go to South America in the fall. The new year to them will mean France until May.

While vagabonding, Mrs. Kapell, 25, arranges everything. Where they'll stay, how long they'll stay, what the children will do, and so forth, come under her planning. She has a faithful list of baby sitters.

Well-Traveled Youngsters

Although Becky, 2, and David, 4, don't go everywhere, they've traveled more than the average oldster. Mrs. Kapell said David traveled 10,000 miles before he was a year old.

REBECCA AND BECKY

She doesn't consider the children much trouble. She even found last Christmas in Philadelphia that they had reached the accomplished travelers' stage when David called room service for two breakfasts while the mother was still

21 East 94th Street: Kapell and his family occupied the first two floors during the years of his marriage. (Below) Kapell in his living room with an unidentified guest; the Picasso he bought with funds borrowed from Fredric Mann hangs over the mantelpiece. (Right) Ten years on, Kapell renews his contract with Arthur Judson as Anna Lou looks on.

Kapell Grows Musically

By MILES KASTENDIECK

William Kapell gave a provocative recital in Town Hall last night. Having apparently taken stock of himself, he appears to have set his sights in a direction somewhat different from the one in which he had been traveling. His performance challenged the listener to reappraise his achievement.

In the three years since he was last heard here as a recitalist, this young pianist has gained musical poise. He must no longer regard playing as a tour-de-force. He is looking beyond the glitter of virtuosity for its own sake and looking into interpretation for the sake of the music. That is real growth.

He has always been a remarkable pianist technically. His firm fingers and his self-assurance, however, had led him to make this accomplishment more of an end than a means to an end. A more sensitive touch and a greater variety of tonal coloring at once suggested last night that he has widened his scope.

There were times when he was still too positive for his own good—too energetic, too percussive, and too rigid, but there was a leavening influence at work to keep him from going too much to excess. It expressed itself in each of the four works which made up his program.

The opening Bach D Major Paritita had definite character beyond clarity of form and of execution. Copland's Sonata (1941) gained substance because Kapell was temperamentally adjusted to it and knew how to make it effective. Debussy's "Children's Corner" and Liszt's Hungarian Rhapsody No. 11 acquired their respective individualities by reason of his interest in style as well as in well-adjusted sounds.

One of the high points of the recital was the second movement of the Copland. He had overdone the percussive element of the first movement, making his tone as hard as nails; but in the second he achieved a balance and a sensitivity quite illuminating.

Kapell seems to have crossed the threshold into new territory where he may use his outstanding talent for finer things. This recital promises a much more interesting pianist.

KAPELL IS HEARD IN PIANO RECITAL

Town Hall Program Includes Liszt 11th Rhapsody, Copland Sonata and Bach Partita

For the last few years one has been wondering if William Kapell was going to be a permanent member of the "promising" group of younger pianists. Of his innate talent there never was any doubt. The question concerned the direction in which he was headed: sterility and mannerism versus musicianship and imagination. His concert last night in Town Hall did much to resolve the issue.

It showed that Mr. Kapell is on his way toward becoming one of the great pianists. It showed a clarification of the emotional problems that must have beset him, and it showed a maturity far in advance of anything he has displayed in this city.

This maturity was reflected in his program. Artistry involves a knowledge of what not to play even more than a knowledge of what to play. Too many young pianists rush to program music with which they have no emotional affinity. In the past Mr. Kapell has been guilty of this offense. Last night, though, he confined his attention to four pieces—Bach's D major Partita, the Copland Sonata, Debussy's "Children's Corner" and Liszt's Eleventh Rhapsody.

These pieces he understood. They were polished, they had proportion and finesse, and they were possessed of musical understanding. In addition, they sang out—and a singing tone in the past has been a rare experience at a Kapell recital.

Of this pianist's perfect mechanism, no more need be said than that nothing bothers him, from the contrapuntal lines of Bach, to the awkward skips of Copland. His Bach could have served as a blueprint of the score, so meticulous was it. Interpretively, the Partita showed an intelligent, sensitive realization of the musical problems. Details here and there were capable of argument, but they were perfectly consistent with his central thesis, which combined a virile approach with an unexpected mixture of lyricism.

The Copland Sonata received a big interpretation; one with power, drive and all the technique in the world. This listener has never heard a performance to match it, and it is not Mr. Kapell's fault if time has stripped off most of what little meat originally covered the music's bones.

Some curious things were noticed in Mr. Kapell's version of Debussy's little suite. The playing commanded respect for its superb control, but the mood of the music was a little too restrained. The pianist adopted almost a sotto-voce attack, obviously determined to hold himself in check if it was the last thing he did (through, inconsistently, there was quite a flurry in the concluding "Golliwog").

In any case, agree or disagree, there was no doubt at all that a real pianist was at the keyboard—a pianist with wonderful fingers, imagination, musical honesty, and an ability to command the entire attention of an audience. Mr. Kapell's emotional range is still capable of expansion, but if last night's recital is any criterion, it will not be long before he expands sufficiently to satisfy the most captious listener.

—H. C. S.

A sampling of Kapell's later hometown press. H.C.S. is Harold Schonberg from the *Times*; F.D.P. is Francis Perkins from the *Herald Tribune*; Kastendieck wrote for the New York *Sun*. Arthur Berger, represented here with a review he wrote for the *Herald Tribune*, went on to become a distinguished composer and educator.

MAY 2?, 1951

CONCERT AND RECITAL

Samaroff Memorial

William Kapell and the members of the Juilliard String Quartet contributed their services last night for the second annual concert at Town Hall in memory of Olga Samaroff, who died three years ago. Mr. Kapell, who was a pupil of this distinguished pianist and teacher, opened the program with Chopin's sonata in B minor. Robert Mann and Robert Koff, violinists; Raphael Hillyer, violist, and Arthur Winograd, cellist, played Beethoven's quartet in C-sharp minor, Op. 131, and were heard with Mr. Kappel in Schumann's quintet in E flat for piano and strings.

A general spirit of devotion marked the performances of these three masterpieces. In the sonata Mr. Kappel was in impressive technical form; energy was a slightly too prominent characteristic in the performance of the first movement, but there was interpretative persuasiveness in his playing of the more lyric measures of the music, including the largo, which he had dedicated to his teacher. The interpretation of the Beethoven quartet was lucid and laudably proportioned, although it did not always fully realise the expressive resources of this work. Good dynamic balance between the piano and the other instruments characterized the performance of the Schumann quintet. The proceeds of the well attended concert will be used for the grants which the Olga Samaroff Foundation provides for talented young pianists in the schools with which Mme. Samaroff was associated at the time of her death, the Juilliard School and the Philadelphia Conservatory of Music. — P.D.P.

CONCERT AND RECITAL

By Arthur Berger

WILLIAM KAPELL
TOWN HALL
Recital last night with the following program:
Partita in D major...........................Bach
Sonata (1941).........................Aaron Copland
Children's Corner.........................Debussy
Hungarian Rhapsody, No. 11..................Liszt

A Pianist Comes of Age

An advance glance at the flyer announcing William Kapell's Town Hall recital last night was enough to give one a premonition that a change has come over this remarkable young pianist, for some time now a candidate for the stellar bracket. But one had to sit the evening through to feel the powerful impact of the immensely gratifying transformation that has taken place. Mr. Kapell's phenomenal dexterity is no news. He could have coasted along on this, showing off his fleet and steely fingers, his extraordinary co-ordination in the few standard pieces that seem to be the domain of the top virtuosos. But he seems to have decided that music, too, is important, and not simply how brilliantly and impressively he plays, but what he plays, too. And with this has come an amazing growth in sensitivity, in the care for phrase and line, in the ability to show not only finger strength, but a tender and loving approach to the music.

Mr. Kapell made only the slightest obeisance to the standard display pieces in his final offering, Liszt's Hungarian Rhapsody, No. 11. But even this received musically elegant treatment, as well as the most glittering manipulation in maters of touch and the execution of passage-work. His central work, however, was a sonata by Copland, rather than any of the standard pieces, and it is a massive, inspired achievement of our time that is altogether worthy of the position in a program that is normally filled by the great sonatas of the past. Though Bach was the familiar composer of the opening work, his Partita in D major is also a rarity.

Substantial thought had obviously gone into the problem of evoking the essential style of each, and it was altogether evident that since his last recital here three years ago, Mr. Kapell has emerged into one of our finest interpreters. It is a good thing for young men to take some time off for reflection and for consolidating their gifts, and Mr. Kapell's example is most convincing. Everything he did showed how much he has escaped falling into routine, and how much distinction he has acquired. The arioso passages of the Bach unfolded in single, exquisitely sustained lines, with every detail, every ornament, carefully accounted for. The rhetoric of the Copland, the brooding sentiments, as if a wasteland is being sadly contemplated, had an overwhelming and deeply moving effect. Then, with keen theatrical sense, he turned out the miniatures of Debussy's "Children's Corner" in a delicate, cameo-like frame of which we had never before thought him capable. It all added up to one of the most striking evenings of piano-playing in our memory.

Young Artists Back Bach, Kapell Says

By DORIS RENO
Herald Music And Art Editor

America's serious young artists are rapidly deserting the Shostakovich-Khatchaturian musical camp to plump for Bach, late Mozart, Beethoven and Schubert, according to William Kapell, 29-year-old pianist, who will play with University of Miami symphony Sunday and Monday.

Kapell, who characterizes Shostakovich and Khatchaturian as "pure, empty bombast," is rejoicing greatly that the "young trend" is back to the beauty and nobility of the classics.

"My performing friends of my own age know it's what you have inside, not what you know or even what you can do, that counts," said the young pianist.

Kapell says he has many friends among the well-known virtuosi of the older generation, and they have plenty of talent — great genius," but he regrets that money has taken precedence with so many of them.

He feels that the state of criticism in this country aids and abets fakery and the show-off type of virtuosity, "for there are very few critics who care whether a pianist is playing his heart out, or not so long as he glitters."

He says empty recitals are praised everywhere, so that a well-known virtuoso can get magnificent reviews for just wiggling his fingers—and that not necessarily on the right notes.

The young pianist, who will play Prokofiev's Third Piano Concerto here with University of Miami Symphony Orchestra expresses himself as fond of "early Prokofiev, Hindemith, and some of Copland, but otherwise my vote goes to the Bach partitas, the works of Schubert's final great period, and Beethoven's Opus 111." Late Mozart, he says, is the consummation of great music for him.

"The works of Liszt, Rachmaninoff, et al, are built around glamor," he contends, "and the young generation of performers is not going for that any more."

Kapell will perform with the university orchestra under John Bitter at 8:30 p.m. Sunday in Miami Beach auditorium and the same time Monday in Dade county auditorium.

During The Week... As I See It

By LEO MINDLIN

Last weekend, I watched the birth of a musician's performance. The young American pianist, William Kapell, sat in his uncle's home at an old, battered upright and pounded his fingers on springless keys until their ends fairly hurt him. Outside, cries of approval were voiced from time to time for the feats of a muscular giant then performing before the Spinoza Forum.

Dr. Abraham Wolfson, a lean and sprightly man, flitted silently about with the vegetarian's goodies in his hand, offering refreshment whenever his nephew paused from practicing or during lulls of our conversation. Sin and virtue became a momentary topic of discussion after Mr. Kapell and I were warned not to smoke so much.

"But virtue, as it never will be moved... so lust... will sate itself in a celestial bed," the pianist quoted from Hamlet. "There's the problem," he said. "Virtue has been moved. Music in our time is performed for other reasons than art — money, I mean. Feeling and heart are commodities to be sold in the concert market."

Mr. Kapell resumed practicing difficult and tiring exercises. For an instant he fell upon a Mozart sonata, cursed himself rather soundly (the Mozart seemed too simple by comparison; he was begging the issue at hand) and returned to the endless chords, runs and arpeggios. Occasional technical misplayings, he rehearsed again and again, until it seemed that the instrument groaned before his demands.

"There must be sincerity somewhere," I said, and made mention of several world famous artists. Mr. Kapell denied that any of them had the true musician's feeling, interrupted himself with a hacking smoker's cough and added that although some had arrived at peerless perfection, none sought such competence except as a means of personal glorification. "You single out Heifetz," he explained. Mr. Kapell had referred earlier to his own recording with the violinist of Brahms' D minor sonata. "There's a man who's no musician but an instrumentalist. Of course, he represents Perfection, but it is perfection for the sake of Haifetz. Feeling makes the difference between artistry and commercial inanity." "Willy's too impetuous," he sighed. "The cigarettes make him so." Mr. Kapell laughed. "He asked me who was the greatest interpreter of Beethoven, and I said Rudolf Serkin. Precisely there lies the problem. Why should he be angry with me?"

Mr. Kapell's personal pianistic development speaks well for the theory he espouses regarding sincerity among musicians and in the arts, generally. I considered our hasty words over the loss of morality in the face of materialism. His own activity in concert circles seems to indicate a growth toward musical refinement. Even as a host of pianists and violinists had begun trading on the mass appeal of late nineteenth and twentieth century Russian romanticism, Mr. Kapell turned to discover the deceptive simplicity and musical genius of Mozart and Bach.

It is a truism that imitators of romantic art inevitably reduce the original intent of such art to bourgeois pomposity and tastelessness. Examples abound of once fine musicians who have turned to performing obviously inferior works for the purpose of enriching themselves. Thus, they are guilty of compromising their ability and fostering ignorance. The plethora of recordings which pretend to immortalize stuttering composers are a case in point, while Artur Rubinstein, among others, is an example of a man who has turned from sincerity to the glitter of popularity and depressed musical standards.

Mr. Kapell admits readily to the error of his beginning ways on the world concert stage. With obvious dissatisfaction, as we drove earlier through the crowded streets of Miami Beach, he emphasized his complete contempt for Aram Khachaturian's Piano Concerto. "There's a piece of flash and nothing — a popular work considered brilliant and difficult by the musically naive. I fell for it too, when I was young." (His boyish exuberance made this seem strange.) "A few bars of Mozart are worth the whole concerto."

Mr. Kapell was caught up by my perplexity. I politely remarked that he had made a Victor recording of the Khachaturian work with the late Dr. Serge Koussevitsky and the Boston Symphony Orchestra. His flinching eyes seemed to indicate that he didn't care to be reminded of this sad fact. Whatever the circumstances, Mr. Kapell subsequently turned to the Old Masters. "They really knew what Willy was," Dr. Wolfson said.

In addition to reviews, newspapers published features, interviews and (below right) occasional news stories on Kapell.

Kapell's Dynamic Piano Technique Well Received By By City Audience

William Kapell, young American piano-forte expert was presented by Famous Artists, Ltd., Thursday night at the Auditorium to an audience whose enthusiasm indicated that the pianist's meteoric career has a solid foundation of extensive musical proportions.

The proximity of two pianists appearing on successive nights would naturally prompt a desire to weigh one against the other, but comparisons being what they are today let us consider Mr. Kapell, who is on the crest of the wave and bids fair to remain there for a long time.

The program was skilfull choice to display the electrifying quality of the artist's technique and the dynamic power of his style.

The opening prelude and fugue in A Minor by Bach-Liszt immediately established the full vigor of his tone, and his powerful rhythmic drive coupled with a crispness of touch.

The following sonata in B flat had an unhackneyed quality and that delicate sensitivity to a satisfying exposition of Mozart. The major work on the program was "pictures at an exhibition." The ten movements, which represent the paintings, were played with such vivid tone coloring that no written explanation was needed to conjure up an old castle, children at play, a lumbering ox-cart, the great gate of Kiev and all the other visions created by Moussorgsky.

Two well-contrasted numbers closed the program. Debussy's "sweet bergamasque," with its tuneful and familiar Clair de lune, had a spontaneity and sensitive interpretitive values. The broad sweep of Liszt's Hungarian Phrapsody No. 11 called for a prodigious display of technical power.

There was a descrimination and authority to Mr. Kapell's performance which made one feel that in the field of piano playing a "Daniel is come to judgment."

DOCTORS AID KAPELL
Fevered-Wracked Pianist Triumphant In Concert

"VANCOUVER PROVINCE" 4/18/53

Three doctors backstage at William Kapell's piano concert Thursday night kept the 29-year-old pianist going through the entire concert, and then sent him to his hotel room and bed.

Despite a fever which ran higher than that which his playing produced on the audience, and with a hacking bronchial cough which persisted throughout his program, Kapell played brilliantly and even gave two encores to a demanding crowd of 2000.

When he had finished, his formal "tails" were soaking wet and his dress shirt—starched when he first appeared—was a soggy pulp. The pianist perspired so that the stage itself around the piano bench was damp. He was forced to mop his forehead several times during the evening.

Famous Artists' management, Holly Maxwell and Hugh Pickett, called a doctor to the Auditorium when they first saw Kapell. He insisted on playing despite his illness.

Two doctors in the audience, when they saw his pale face, heard his cough and his efforts to shake perspiration from his eyes, rushed backstage to be on hand.

One Kapell fan left her seat after his first selection and gave the artist some cough medicine which helped some.

Despite it all, Kapell performed with a combination of technical mastery and interpretive flair that literally taxed the resources of his instrument.

The program opened with a surprise: a Liszt transcription of a Bach prelude and fugue, played more in the style of Liszt than Bach. Then a Mozart sonata with birdlike ornamentation, a quality of detached serenity and facile technique that contrived to draw three curtain calls.

The "Pictures at an Exhibition" of Moussorgsky was colorful, clangorous in places, with wide variations showing splendid control, humor, rhythmic depth and brilliant descriptive effects. Too long to describe in detail, it was enough to bring shouts of "Bravo!" among the applause that burst forth.

Kapell's final group was in marked contrast: Debussy's crystal "Suite Bergamasque," followed by the color and drive of the Liszt "Hungarian Rhapsody No. 11," both excellently done. Then two unnamed encores, fragile and lovely, but confusing in that they seemed to blend contemporary styling with romantic construction.—V. P.

Concert Pianist To Talk Back t[o]

By RUTH SULLI[VAN]

William Kapell, young American co[ncert pianist has a] chance to talk back to critics.

Kapell, here for a concert of the Ne[w York Sym]phony Society tomorrow, quoted his frie[nds, one] and all: "They insult us; they embarra[ss us; let's do] something about."

A music critic, Kapell said, [...] should be a combination of a teach[...] er and a policeman.

Many of the members of the pro[...]fession are highly qualified and [...] very sincere in their desire to be [...] closely associated with the art of music. But sometimes the perform[...]er can't help feeling that it would be fine to call a meeting of the crit[...]ics and say, "You said there was [...] not enough wit in such and such a [...] passage. Now just where does th[e] wit come in? Show me on th[e] score."

Cites Chief Danger

A rebel against what he ca[lls] "the ultra-conformist era we're [in] now," Kapell, who has been [con]certizing since he was 17, s[aid,] "The chief danger today is o[ur] musical conformism.

"Audiences and symphony [man]agers would hold one down t[o] old chestnuts, to be played ov[er and] over. This is retarding the [devel]opment of music in Ameri[ca as in] every other country today.

"There is splendid pian[o music] by Hindemuth, Copland, [...] and Bartok, but no one [wants to] listen to it. This provides [a deter]rent to the contemporary [composer,] of course, since he wants [to be] heard."

There is, he finds, a [...]

KAPELL MANNER FAILS TO PLEASE

But His Piano Technique Draws Praise

By CHARLOTTE UPTON

William Kapell stopped off in Spokane last night long enough to give a concert classical in its perfection, brevity, program and technique.

There is no question about Kapell's virtuosity—he has brilliance, technique and lyric beauty. However, his manner seemed to baffle many of his listeners. Perhaps the audience got off on the wrong foot by applauding between movements in the Mozart sonata. He was surprised. In fact, he seemed surprised that he had an audience at all—much as a self-effacing, but haughty music teacher might be startled to discover that he was not alone while playing his favorite selections.

Flattered Audience

He played three short encores without announcing them, thereby flattering his audience by assuming that everyone knew them, the only unfamiliar parts of a standard repertoire.

The young American pianist opened with Bach's Prelude and Fugue in A Minor. The prelude is often referred to as Bach's "Moonlight Sonata," while the fugue is considered one of his most skillful.

The Mozart Sonata in B-Flat Major had all the lyrical beauty and deceptively simple precision one associates with Mozart and expects from the masters of his interpretation, as Kapell undoubtedly is.

Deleted Schumann

Chopin's Sonata in B Minor concluded the first half of the program. Like Chopin's other two piano sonatas, this consisted of four independent compositions linked arbitrarily together. Chopin always has audience appeal, especially when played as Kapell did it last night.

He departed from his scheduled program by substituting Debussy's Children's Suite (Children's Corner) for Schumann's Scenes of Childhood. Both the familiarity and the childhood element would have been there, but the original choice would have left more scope for imagination and variety of interpretation.

The Hungarian Rhapsody No. 11 by Liszt ended the pr[ogram...]

★—★—★—★—★

wants to do and behaves the way he wants to behave. I can't believe this is a wholesome atmosphere for any artist."

Doesn't Like Selection

Kapell, who scored a great international success with his recording of the Khatchaturian piano concerto, smiled briefly when questioned about it.

"I never play it any more, and haven't in five years. I just don't like it. It doesn't wear well."

Tomorrow night he will play the Prokofieff piano concerto, with Alexander Hilsberg conducting the orchestra.

This morning he was doctoring a bad cough acquired yesterday. "This happens all the time. Whenever I get a slight cold, it turns into the worst cough you ever heard."

He was confident, however, that the cough would not interfere with tomorrow night's concert.

WILLIAM KAPELL

Not all the reviews were favorable and, unlike many artists who suffer in silence, Kapell was quite happy to disagree publicly with his critics. The review of a 1951 Toronto recital (right) is particularly interesting in that it was written by Alberto Guerrero, the only professional teacher with whom Glenn Gould studied.

Music in Toronto
Kapell Program At Massey Hall Conservative

By ALBERTO GUERRERO

William Kapell, recognized as one of the most brilliant virtuosi of the young generation of American pianists, played at Massey Hall last night.

This was his first complete recital in Toronto, but musical audiences know him well for his appearances with the TSO. In fact, I would imagine that few listeners, unless they dislike modern idioms altogether, will ever forget his sensational performance of the Katchaturian Concerto some three or four seasons ago.

His program last night was a conservative one, and those who had hoped that the visit of an outstanding interpreter of today's American musical thought was a marvellous opportunity to hear the new music genuinely played, were out of luck.

The concerto started with the Partita in D major by Bach, a suite of pieces written, most of them, in dance rhythms. Of these dances, the Allemande seemed of an extraordinary length. A richly ornamented cantilena unfolds itself over a harmonic structure that, though full of connecting and prolonged links, maintains an ample and far-reaching unity of purpose. The pianist seemed to have put all his attention in the ornamented cantilena upon which he lavished his most delicate pianissimos and varied tonal effects.

At that moment, I agreed with Bach's contemporary, Rameau, who thought that the musical expression was really to be found in the harmony. It is also interesting to note that it was in the Sarabande that perhaps the freer rubato of the evening appeared in the form of a considerable enlargement of the first phrase.

The Chopin Sonata was brilliantly played, with great tonal contrasts in the style of the real virtuoso. After two or three minutes of pianissimo in the slow movement, for instance, the thunder of the female seemed terrifying: all extremely well thought out and most efficiently done.

The Children's Corner Finale by Debussy was exquisitely presented, the delicacy of the playing fitting to perfection the subtleties of the texture. Altogether a remarkable recital and

23, CAVENDISH CLOSE,
N.W.8

August 4th 1952

Dear William

Your modest reminder of our first meeting with Sascha Grenier recalls that evening vividly; in fact I have never forgotten how you gave me courage for my first concert in New York after the war.

I was full of apprehension fearing that you young people would find my playing "old fashioned", but when you said: "We are going to hear something we have been waiting for." (I believe those are your very words!) I was reassured & deeply touched.

And so this letters begins in 1940 & continues with my gratitude for your very lovely letter of July 6th. I am sorry not to have written to you sooner, but the word "holiday" seems to have vanished from my vocabulary.

Admiring letters from great artists such as Myra Hess meant more to Kapell than most reviews.

> I would not miss a Casals Festival for anything in the world, but it means virtually working all the year through, especially as I again playing here in September.
>
> As this will probably be repeated next year, I am afraid it will be impossible to contemplate any teaching, & I regret so much that I cannot take your gifted pupil.
>
> It is a real grief to me that for so many years now, this wretched life of concert giving has prevented my having the pleasure of working with young artists. I am always hoping that it will be possible one day, & my recording is in the same situation of "ifs and whens"!! Do tell your pupil how sorry I am — Perhaps I will hear him some time.
>
> Thank you again for your letter & all my warmest wishes to the three of you — (you haven't grown a beard again I hope?!!)
>
> Yours ever sincerely
> Myra Hess

11200 Sunset Blvd.
West Los Angeles.   L. A.   Sept. 17.
Calif.

WILLIAM KAPELL

Dear Virgil,
 I am planning, in the season 1953-4, 2 concerts devoted entirely to American Piano music. I would very much like suggestions as to what to include of yours. There are several things I am fond of, but you may have something to which you partial. If so, I would like to see it.

As it is shaping up in my mind at present, I will play works by yourself, Sessions, Copland, Ives, and possibly Ruggles. Too, there will be represented a member of my generation; who it shall be I don't know yet. I shall go through quite a bit a music before making a decision on that point.

I want it to be an important representation of our music, and, unfortunately, some famous names will not be on the program, simply because I have no particular sympathy for their piano works. However, it would be impossible, and not a little undiscriminating to play works by everybody. In any case, when I return to N.Y. we can discuss this at greater length. I plan to play one work which is purely "virtuoso", but have not found many, aside from some of your Etudes.

One critic whom Kapell particularly respected was Virgil Thomson, the chief critic of the New York *Herald Tribune* from 1940 to 1954, and a leading composer. This letter to Thomson, dating from the late summer of 1952, reflects Kapell's lifelong interest in American music.

> It seems to me a crying shame that some of the fine pieces in our native literature are not played more often. If we allow the present and lamentable accent on commerce and denationalism to continue, our whole musical culture will be threatened. The situation today appears very serious, and no little bit tragic. The powers that control this noble profession are making nit-wits out of the large public. A public not interested in active participation at a concert, but a dull, complacent, and uncultivated mass of grey. I, for one, am sick and tired of going along in any way with the public "taste." Many artists do not realize that by doing so they slowly are dying, creatively; and when artists die, so does Art.
>
> When I return to the East, I shall record Copland's Sonata, your enchanting "Ten Easy Pieces," and one work of my friend Abram Chasins. I would have done them here, but the studio is dry, and I couldn't get a satisfactory sound. So I'll wait till I can have Town Hall again. Aaron's Sonata, I love, and have wanted to record it for some time. All these projected plans are, of course, over R.C.A. Victor's disinterested protests.
>
> We have had a nice summer; I have been playing a good deal with Joseph Schuster here at home, he is a superb artist.
>
> I hope you have had a good vacation. Do let me hear from you. We leave here on Oct. 13.
>
> Warm regards
>
> Willy

The hands of William Kapell. (Inset) Kapell's final season of concerto appearances.

ORCHESTRAS — 1952-1953

WILLIAM KAPELL

NOV. 5	ST. PAUL	RACHMANINOFF, C MINOR
NOV. 27-28	N.Y. PHIL.	MOZART, K.453 ✓
DEC. 1	DALLAS	BRAHMS, D MINOR ✓
DEC. 9	NEW ORLEANS	PROKOFIEFF NO. 3
DEC. 14-15	PITTSBURGH	BRAHMS, D MINOR
DEC. 19-20	BOSTON	PROKOFIEFF
DEC. 26-27	PHILA. ORCH.	BRAHMS, D MINOR
DEC. 29	PHILA. ORCH.	MOZART, K.414, PROKOFIEFF
DEC. 30	PHILA. ORCH. — N.Y.	MOZART, K.414, PROKOFIEFF
JAN. 6	PHILA. ORCH. — WASH.	MOZART, K.414, PROKOFIEFF
JAN. 7	PHILA. ORCH. BALT.	MOZART, K.414, PROKOFIEFF
JAN. 27-28	MONTREAL	PROKOFIEFF
FEB. 1-3	BUFFALO	RACHMANINOFF, D MINOR
FEB. 10	CHICAGO	BRAHMS, D MINOR
FEB. 12-13	CHICAGO	RACHMANINOFF, D MINOR
FEB. 23	PHILA. ORCH. YOUTH	PROKOFIEFF
APRIL 11-12	N.Y. PHIL.	PROKOFIEFF

The Dallas Symphony Orchestra
INCORPORATED

2310 South Lamar St. • Dallas 2, Texas • IMperial 1579
WALTER HENDL, Musical Director • MORGAN KNOTT, Manager

December 8, 1952

Personal

Mr. William Kapell
c/o Columbia Artists Management, Inc.
113 West 57th Street
New York 19, New York

Dear Willy:

I have come to the conclusion that you are the great American pianist; ditto me as conductor. Why the hell don't we keep in touch with each other from time to time from now on?

Affectionately,

Walter

Walter Hendl

WH:c

P.S.—Knocked out Virgil Thomson with a concert here yesterday.

In the last years of his life, Kapell took up teaching; indeed, at the time of his death, he had agreed to join the piano faculty of the Juilliard School. Three of his students — Philip Leland, Joel Rice and Jerome Lowenthal (the last of whom has written a memoir of his studies with Kapell) —played this informal concert during the summer of 1952 in Los Angeles.

William Kapell
presents
A Student Recital by his Summer Class

Program

One

Liszt — Sonnetto del Petrarca
Chopin — Two Etudes

Philip Leland

Two

Haydn — Sonata, C Major

Jerome Lowenthal

Three

Bach — Partita, D Major

Joel Rice

Intermission

Four

Chopin — Mazurka, G Sharp Minor
Nocturne, F Sharp Minor

Jerome Lowenthal

Five

Copland — Sonata

Joel Rice

Studies for a portrait by John Stewart.

148

Another session with photographer John Stewart, this one at home on East 94th Street.

(Above) Off for an exhilarating tour of Israel in early 1953. (Below) The Kapell family at home during the 1952 holidays.

Three generations of family — photographs taken at Harry and Edith Kapell's home in Florida during Kapell's last visit with his parents in 1953.

Kapell was a late but enthusiastic convert to cigarette smoking, which he adopted in his mid-20s. By 1953, he was a chain smoker and suffered from many of the health problems associated with the habit.

Kapell plays Mozart with Pablo Casals at the monastery of St. Michel de Cuxa, near Prades, in the summer of 1953. Some private recordings made at the festival reflect the pianist's full maturity.

REVISED PROGRAMS FOR MELBOURNE

WILLIAM KAPELL
Pianist

PROGRAM No. 1

Adelaide *Perth* Bach   I.   timings
Sydney

             Suite, A minor (miscellaneous)   7
                Allemande
                Courante
                Sarabande I
                Sarabande II
                Gigue

Melbourne Sydney Perth Moussorgsky   II.

             Pictures at an Exhibition   29-30

             Intermission

Argentine *Sydney M.P.A.* Mozart   III.

             Sonata, C major, K. 330   15

Sydney Adelaide Brisbane Chopin   IV.

             Sonata, Op. 35   20

PROGRAM No. 2

S.M.P.A. Mozart   I.
             Sonata, B-flat, K. 570   15

Melbourne Adelaide Prokofieff   II.
             Sonata, No. 7   17

             Intermission

Israel *Sydney Melbourne Adelaide* Schubert   III.
             Sonata, A major, Op. Posth   31-32

PROGRAM No. 3

Sydney Adelaide Perth Scarlatti   I.
             4 Sonata (Longo ed.)

Copland   II.
Sydney Adelaide Melbourne   Sonata (1941)   22

             Intermission

Debussy *Sydney Adelaide Melbourne*   III.
             Suite Bergamasque   17

Chopin *Sydney Adelaide Perth*   IV.
             Barcarolle   7
             Nocturne E-flat op. 55   5
             Scherzo, B minor   8
             Polonaise Fantasy

Adelaide Perth Sydney Schubert 4 Impromptus   30
Ballarat Newcastle Mozart Sonata A Major K331   15

TITLE

I.
Sonata, C Major
     Mozart

II.
Sonata, No. 7

III.
4 Impromptus
     Schubert
Barcarolle

Sydney?   PROGRAM
Bach   I.

~~Beethoven~~   II.

     Intermi...

Albeniz   III.
(Durand & File, publisher)

PROGRAM No. 5 (light) for s...
Mr. Kapell is wiring Mr. Ja...

He a... that Programs 2, 3 a...
also the movements of the Bac...
rest of Program 1 he has alr...

Ballarat Newcastle Prelude & Fugue
Argentine Schumann Kinderscen...
Argentine Bach Liszt A min...

PROGRAM NO. 3

TIMING	PUBLISHER	
15 minutes	Kalmus	
17 minutes	Leeds	*Melbourne* *Adelaide*
INTERMISSION		
30 minutes	Schirmer	*Adelaide* *Perth*
7 minutes	Kalmus	*Adelaide* *Perth*

Kapell worked out the programs for his long Australian tour with his customary care.

William Kapell

PROGRAME NO. 1

TITLE	TIMING	PUBLISHER	
I. Sonata – Copland	22 minutes	Boosey and Hawkes	*Sydney recital* *Melbourne Recital* *Adelaide*
II. Nocturne, Op. 55, E Flat – Chopin	5 minutes	Kalmus	
Polonaise-Fantasie – Chopin	12 minutes	Kalmus	*Sydney recital* *Melbourne* *Adelaide*
INTERMISSION			
III. Sonata, A Major – Schubert	32 minutes	Kalmus – *Recital Melbourne* *Sydney* *Adelaide*	

Brahms D Minor – Brisbane
– Sydney
Philadelphia Ormandy –

Partita, D major
Sonata, Op. 14, No.1   36
                          16

Rondeña
Malagueña   *perhaps*   7
Navarra   *encores*   3
                              5

l follow.
oncertos

to Mr. James
ram 1. The
r. James

Bach 7/0

THE AUSTRALIAN BROADCASTING COMMISSION

presents the

Queensland Symphony Orchestra

IN THE SIXTH CONCERT
OF THE 1953 SUBSCRIPTION SERIES

Guest Conductor:
Joseph Post

Soloist:
William Kapell
Pianist

★

BRISBANE CITY HALL

FRIDAY, 21st AUGUST — AT 8 P.M.
SATURDAY, 22nd AUGUST — AT 8 P.M.

★

This Series of Concerts is arranged by the Australian Broadcasting Commission in conjunction with the Queensland State Government and the Brisbane City Council.

QUEENSLAND SYMPHONY ORCHESTRA

1953

Direction:
THE AUSTRALIAN BROADCASTING COMMISSION

William Kapell

William Kapell, young American pianist who first electrified Australian audiences with his dazzling technique in 1945, is now acknowledged in the U.S.A. as one of the foremost pianists. In recent years his musical development and increasing artistic maturity have earned him glowing tributes from leading American critics, who have described him as "one of the great pianists."

"A mature, superbly disciplined pianist, who is only incidentally a virtuoso," wrote another critic recently.

Since his first Australian visit he has been in constant demand, touring the United States annually. He has also appeared throughout Europe, including concerts in such centres as Budapest, Oslo, Stockholm, Copenhagen, Rome, Milan, Brussels, The Hague and London, and has made three tours of South America.

Before leaving for Australia this year he completed his tenth sold-out tour of America. This season he had the signal honour of appearing twice as soloist with the New York Philharmonic Orchestra under Mitropoulos—the first time the Philharmonic has invited a pianist to play twice in the same season.

Just before his arrival in Australia he completed a tour of Israel, giving recitals, and appearing with the Israel Philharmonic Orchestra.

Kapell is interested in playing works by what he calls the old masters of tomorrow—in other words our contemporaries. He says he tries to achieve two things in his playing; first, a beautiful singing tone, and second, to recreate what the composer felt when he wrote the music.

Among the latest American critiques of his playing have been the following comments:—

"A masterly performance."—New York Herald Tribune.

"He brought strength, brilliance and poetic feeling to rhapsodic music. The audience applauded him tumultuously."—New York Times.

Annotations

1. OVERTURE—"FIDELIO" — Beethoven (1770-1827)

Few operas have aroused such controversy as Beethoven's single contribution to the stage, "Fidelio," first entitled "Leonora." At one end are those belittling the score as purely "symphonic" rather than "operatic;" at the other, Beethoven devotees, among them highly respected conductors and singers, ranking it at the very top of the repertory.

But, as Louis Biancolli writes in his programme notes for the Philharmonic-Symphony Society of New York, "if the opera itself has stirred up aesthetic strife, what shall be said of the tangle of conflict and confusion caused by 'Fidelio's' four overtures? The chronology and appropriateness of all four have been freely argued over, and a fat volume could be made of the scholarly pros and cons. In 1924 Josef Braunstein's keen analysis of the overtures appeared to clinch the issue of chronological order. The numbering of the 'Leonora' overtures is now accepted as correct in its given sequence; that is, No. 1 really came first (actually a discarded attempt); No. 2 second (played at the first production of the opera in 1805; No. 3 third (played at the second production in 1806, for which Beethoven had revised the whole work), and "Fidelio" (composed for the final revision of the opera in 1814) last. On the other hand, the biographer Thayer believed the first 'Leonora' Overture was written for a concert in Prague in 1807, which did not take place."

The story of the opera is as follows: Florestan, a noble Spaniard, has aroused the enmity of Pizarro, who holds him prisoner in a fortress of which he is the governor, with the intention of bringing about his death. Leonora, Florestan's wife, dons masculine attire and, as Fidelio, obtains employment as assistant to Rocco, the jailer. Pizarro orders the latter to slay the prisoner. Meeting with refusal, he prepares to do so himself, when Leonora throws herself between them, and threatens him with a pistol. At this moment a trumpeter on the ramparts announces the approach of the Minister of State. Florestan is saved.

The Overture begins with an Allegro section, in which the principal subject is foreshadowed by strings and woodwind. A slow section follows, suggesting the long days and nights spent in prison by Florestan. This is based on two melodies, the first being given out by the horn, the second by the clarinet. The Allegro returns, and is followed by another Adagio section. After a dramatic climax, the Overture proper is reached, the principal theme of the Allegro is given out by the horns and taken up by the clarinet. The second subject is stated by the strings. These themes are developed and the Overture comes to an end with a vigorous Coda.

2. CONCERTO No. 1 in D MINOR, Op. 15 — Brahms
for Pianoforte and Orchestra (1833-1897)

Maestoso;
Adagio;
Rondo (Allegro non troppo)

Soloist: WILLIAM KAPELL

Brahms' two great pianoforte concertos rank amongst the highest achievements of any composer in this form and are both written on such a large scale as to fit the description of symphonies with obligato solo instrument rather than that of their academic title of solo concertos with orchestra.

"It is well enough known," as Neville Cardus once wrote, "that the first two movements of the D Minor Concerto emerged from the composer's first essay to write a symphony, and that the Maestoso (First Movement) was inspired by the news of Schumann's attempt to commit suicide. But it is not so well understood that when a fact or happening in the external universe enters the creative imagination of an artist, it becomes something entirely different. For years, the D Minor Concerto was held to be 'austere,' great but 'forbidding.' The obvious truth is that it contains not only music of deep thoughtfulness and tragic overtones, but also one or two of the most genial and rippling melodies in existence, not to mention the infectious rhythms of the Rondo finale, in which the first notes of the second melody are transformed to such horn music as seems to come sounding from all the misty woods of romance.

ONE RECITAL ONLY

William Kapell

Kapell has the grand manner of Rubinstein and the fingers of Horowitz . . . He is one of the great pianists.—*Chicago Tribune.*

There was no doubt at all that a real pianist was at the keyboard . . . . William Kapell played with magnificent artistry.—*New York Times.*

To his fabulous technique he has been adding reams of poetic interpretation in the past two or three seasons.—*World Telegram and Sun.*

★

CITY HALL — BRISBANE

WEDNESDAY, 26th AUGUST, AT 8.15 P.M.

Programme will include:

Sonata Op. 35 (Chopin).

Suite in A Minor (Bach);

Sonata in C Major K. 330 (Mozart);

Pictures at an Exhibition (Moussorgsky);

★

BOX PLANS NOW OPEN AT PALINGS AND A.B.C.

PRICES: RES. 15/-, 12/6, 10/-, 7/6, 5/- PLUS TAX

Direction:
AUSTRALIAN BROADCASTING COMMISSION

ANNOTATIONS—(Continued)

"So even in the first movement, gloomy and black at the beginning, with a fortissimo D thundering over a roll of drums; soon the clouds disperse and, after piano trills which call for both strength and delicacy, we hear a song of consolation, a beautiful example of writing for the solo instrument. And the cadence gives the horn player another golden chance in its echoes and its lovely fall of an octave.

"In the Adagio complete nonsense is made of the old saying that Brahms could not display or disclose the true quality of the piano. Here is a challenge to soft expressive and reflective touch and tone. Also we are given an example of an orchestral diminuendo without a peer in all music.

"It is always difficult to remember that this gigantic composition, so rich in variety of nature, ranging from tragedy and wise resignation to fancy and exuberance, should have come from a young man of twenty-five years old. But Brahms was always mature; he had no artistic adolescence. He was the soloist in the first performance of the concerto in Leipzig in January, 1858, conducted by Joachim. The audience hissed the work. And young Brahms wrote of this dismaying experience (and he, of course, knew the music as we know it to-day) in these terms: 'The failure has made no impression on me. After all, I am only experimenting and feeling my way.' A classic example of the modesty of genius."

— INTERVAL —

3. SYMPHONY—"MATHIS der MALER" — Hindemith (1895-)

Engelkonzert (Angelic Concert);
Grablegung (The Entombment);
Versuchung des heiligen Antonius (The Temptation of Saint Anthony).

This work was first performed under Furtwangler in March, 1934, at a Berlin Philharmonic concert, and is in reality a joining together of three excerpts from Hindemith's opera of the same name. The subject of the opera is the sixteenth century German painter, Matthias Grunewald, and the three movements that constitute the symphony refer to three sections of a triptych which he painted for the Isenheim altar at Colmar in Alsace. Matthias Grunewald, as he has been known for the last two-and-a-half centuries, was born, as research has only recently discovered, about 1460 in Wurzburg, and his name was, in fact, Mathias Gothart Nithart, though the "Nithart" is no more than a nickname added to his fine patronymic in virtue of his stern, warlike character. He was court painter in turn to two Prince Archbishops, and his leanings towards the Reformation (he fought on the side of the Peasants in the Peasants' War) cost him his place in the Archbishop Albrecht's service, as Hindemith relates in the opera. That was in 1526. Besides his masterpiece, the Isenheim Altar, commissioned by the Brotherhood of Saint Anthony, which is one of the finest pieces of German mediaeval painting, he is known to have painted in Aschaffenburg, Seligenstadt, Frankfurt and Mainz, and his best known works are in Munich, Stuppach, Karlsruhe, and Basle, all on sacred subjects. Of his last years little is known except that he died in humble circumstances, his painting abandoned for the simpler craft of building watermills, in 1528.

In some programme notes on this work, Strobel, a distinguished German musical critic and essayist, wrote: "When Paul Hindemith combined three excerpts from his opera, 'Mathis der Maler' and called the result a 'symphony,' the term did not imply a symphonic construction as understood by the Nineteenth Century. These tone-pieces do not embody a definite 'symphonic idea.' They are not related in theme, but are based instead on 'themes' suggested by the Isenheim Altar of Grunewald. The Symphony has nothing whatever in common with programme-music of the customary descriptive sort. Hindemith excludes any pictorial intention, and dispenses with dramatizing colour effects, changing the sound-material in accordance with purely musical laws. The transformation of the emotional tension into purely musical effects is further increased by the circumstance that in the first part, 'Angelic Concert,' and in the third part, 'The Vision of the Temptation of Saint Anthony,' old church melodies are used. These ancient melodies constitute the true germ-cell music; they determine its melodic and harmonic tissue. The development of the three movements is singularly clear. The dynamic curve descends from the festive and happy Angelic Concert at the beginning to the quiet elegy of the Entombment, and then proceeds, after the music of the Saint's ordeal, to the concluding Hallelujah Hymn of the final visionary exaltation."

Kapell plays one of his recordings for Anna Lou and David.

The last photographs of
Kapell and Anna Lou —
Australia, Summer 1953.

WILLIAM KAPELL - AUSTRALIAN TOUR - 1953

"The poet who resides behind Mr. Kapell's waistcoat...took full control at last night's solo recital at the Capitol. My goodness! How that poet has grown in the seven years since Kapell played here last! Kapell has developed from a brilliant young man into an artist who is even more brilliant where brilliance is in place, but who now grips imagination and heart with grand performances of mature power and outstanding artistic integrity. From first to last, no matter whither the programme led, we had that deeply satisfying evidence of proportion and balance, exquisitely expressed, which is one mark of a first-class artist. And we had a constant assurance that with Kapell the composer comes first, that the performer never stands, with mere effect-making, between the composer and ourselves...We cannot recall a performance which measured up to all this so splendidly as did Mr. Kapell's. ...In s   t, Mr. Kapell has become an artist whom we must place among the outstanding pianists of our experience over many years." "Fidelio," Perth

"Uncommonly attractive playing...It was a rare delight to hear a Mozart concerto played with the aristocratic polish and well bred charm which Kapell brought to the music." John Moses, Sydney

"William Kapell is the first contemporary minded top-rank pianist to tour Australia. His Melbourne concert season, which opened at the Town Hall on Saturday night, could not have been better timed. Its importance cannot be overestimated...In the sense that few living pianists have William Kapell's automatic command of muscular reflex, the performance was more than sensational - it was possibly unique. At no time, however, was there a suspicion of mere gymnastic cleverness. Only the results registered." Biddy Allen, Melbourne "Argus"

"He justified a claim to rank among the world's most rewarding pianists. Not that this young American merely copies the older virtuosos. On the contrary. Nothing could be more individual than the relaxed, seemingly effortless way he played Rachmaninov's Piano Concerto No. 3...Wonderful clarity and control marked even the most difficult passages in Kapell's playing. And the concerto's romantic feeling was charmingly but not over-sentimentally, conveyed. Delicacy of feeling was again the soloist's strong point in Mozart's Piano Concerto in G, as he steered nicely between a too cold and a effusive manner. ...We had Kapell, and that was an event." Arthur Jacobs, Daily Telegraph, Sydney

This Clipping From
BOSTON, MASS.
Christian Science Monitor
SEP 12 1953

Kapell Plays Copland Music In Melbourne

By Biddy Allen
Melbourne

The winter concert season here was marked by two memorable interpretations. William Kapell's treatment of Aaron Copland's Piano Sonata, 1941, was notable both for pliable keyboard technique and for dedicated fervor.

Passionately convinced as to the lasting quality of the music, Kapell approached the task of introduction with self-confessed doubt as to the Australian reception of a work which he conceives it his responsibility to sponsor, although it has had a stormy passage round the musical world. He need not have worried. The patent sincerity of Copland's approach to 20th-century confusion, the aural acceptance of ugly noises as part of an industrial environment, and the determination to achieve and to maintain creative peace of mind by inner discipline, made clear and impressive impact on an audience willing to learn and ready to admire.

Greatest Achievement

This was Kapell's greatest achievement during his Melbourne season. His playing was at all times vital and thought-provoking, but in the Copland Sonata he showed an ability which suggested that he is only at the beginning of his interpretative career.

Hans Schmidt-Isserstedt's conducting of the Brahms D major Symphony was another memorable event. At his first appearance as guest conductor of the Victorian Symphony Orchestra, he showed splendid virility of mind in his interpretations of Beethoven's Fourth Symphony and Hindemith's Concert Piece for Brass and Strings.

Neither performance approached, however, the magnificent appreciation of time, space, and mood apparent from the first note of the Brahms symphony. This was one of those rare and unpredictable performances in which the life pulse of the music asserted its power with the initial breaking of silence.

Absolute Command

Schmidt-Isserstedt has absolute command of punctuation and employs it on a grand scale between symphonic movements. The separation of the four sections in the Brahms example was exceptionally pronounced — the sense of anticipation was correspondingly quickened by such timing and coloring of final notes as necessitated resolution, both rhythmic and tonal, at each fresh entrance.

Only moderate success attended the first Australian stage presentation of Menotti's "The Telephone," sponsored on Aug. 2 by the

---

Although much of the Australian press was good, Kapell was infuriated by some of the reviews he received. The Eunice Gardiner article (below right) would take on a bitter irony in retrospect.

By Eunice Gardiner

The madhatter critics have driven me away

— SAYS WILLIAM KAPELL

WILLIAM KAPELL, visiting American pianist (and one of the world's greatest), swears that when he leaves Australia next week it will be goodbye for ever.

"I shall never return," he told me this week as the climax to a bitter protest against a substantial measure of local criticism of his concerts.

Mr. Kapell said his protest was directed principally — indeed almost wholly — against Mr. Lindsey Browne, music critic of the Sydney Morning Herald.

Kapell told me:

"It is time that a stop was put to the Madhatters' tea-party, which represents a large proportion of music criticism in Sydney.

"Mr. Lindsey Browne, of the Sydney Morning Herald, is the mastermind of a precious coterie of gentlemen who all write, it seems, as he dictates.

"Much of what is written is uninformed, false, and malicious; it is often even ridiculous."

Then Mr. Kapell made his vow never to return here.

"Never" is a big word, and changing circumstances may cause him to relent (and return) in later years.

But right now the world-famous pianist is good and mad and it's as well that the days of duels are done.

For his art demands satisfaction for what has been said about it.

Kapell crouched lower in his armchair and glowered as he swung into the main theme of his interview with me.

It might have been Beecham sitting there, spitting invective; it might have been Beethoven spilling rage. The air was electric.

"Would these critics have people believe that

William Kapell

it means I am working physically and mentally.

"Look: all my concerts begin with music, end with music, and there's music in the middle, too.

"The critics say: 'He began his concert by striding brusquely.'

"They say: 'Dry Bach!' Listen to this. Is it dry?"

The air was filled with liquid sound, mellow, golden, authoritative, as Kapell turned to his keyboard.

He continued: "They say my Schubert sonata had 'surprising warmth.'

"Why surprising? — It doesn't surprise me.

"Schubert's sonatas are some of the most wonderful music in the world.

"They talk of 'tone as hard as New York asphalt'!

"That's a lie—a down-

"Is New York's asphalt harder than any other, anyway?

"The kindest interpretation that can be put on what these men have written about my playing is that they don't know any better.

'Irresponsible'

"But I don't think this is true.

"Even though they aren't musicians, they must have listened to recordings, read about music, studied something of the art.

"I believe that these sort of irresponsible utterances are the result of unprincipled minds.

"They are the words of men who have no sense of responsibility to the art they serve.

"They play with words regardless of their meaning.

"If they chose their words with as much care as I choose the tones I play, they, too, might claim integrity.

"These critics want music to be as limited as their own little minds.

"So—that which is beautiful, that which is true, they damn it—they dismiss.

"When fine art is derided and mediocre work praised—then false standards are set up.

"This is an evil thing and of great danger to the future of music and young musicians in this city of Sydney."

Part Four : Afterwards

*T*he DC-6 smashed into Kings Mountain, just south of San Francisco, at a few minutes before nine on the morning of October 29, 1953. All 19 people on board were killed instantly. Kapell had traveled more than 8000 miles since leaving Australia and was within three minutes of landing in the United States.

Anna Lou had been in the Judson Agency office when Kapell's managers received the news, and noticed a marked change in mood among the people there, but neither Ruth O'Neill, Judson's partner, nor Sascha Greiner, with whom she visited downstairs at Steinway and Sons immediately thereafter, had the courage to tell her what had happened. And so she was told by a trembling Eugene Istomin and Constance Hope, who met her in the lobby of New York's Meurice Hotel, where she and the children were staying awaiting Kapell's return. ("But he has so much left to do!" Anna Lou wept as the elevator ascended.)

Bernard Kapell learned of the accident in Manhattan's Pennsylvania Station. "I went to the newsstand and there it was, in big black letters — 'PLANE CRASHES; William Kapell Feared Dead.' Something very similar happened to my parents. They had moved to Florida and something was the matter with their phone. Fred Mann tried to reach them for hours, without success. Finally, they heard the news over the radio."

Tributes poured in from around the world, several of the most eloquent are presented in full on the following pages. A moving eulogy was delivered the next week by Alistair Cooke in his regular *Letter From America* broadcast over the BBC:

> In a country which tends to make a business, and a profitable one, out of any rare talent, William Kapell held fiercely and unyieldingly to a view of his profession as almost a priesthood, which required unwavering devotion from dawn to midnight;

unremitting practice, practice, practice; an almost trembling humility before good music, ancient and modern....

He died a lucky man. For not many men come into middle age have been fortunate enough to go through to the end without, in some forgivable way, compromising their best. He ended as he began — a cocky, humble apprentice to the master he hoped to be. He left no money, but when the wing of his plane touched that mountain, he went out like Bunyan's pilgrim — undefeated.

For some years after his death, not much was heard about William Kapell. The family lodged a suit against the airline; over the next 15 years, the case was tried, won and then finally overturned. Aaron Copland's Piano Fantasy — the work he had wanted to write for Kapell — was now dedicated to his memory. (It was first performed at the Juilliard School in 1957.)

All of Kapell's recordings went out of print and some of them became highly-sought-after collector's items. Occasionally, a private or "pirate" recording of a Kapell concert would be issued by a small company; far from being displeased, Anna Lou encouraged their proliferation and was delighted whenever a new performance would turn up — as they do, to this day.

I remember my own first encounter with William Kapell's work, as a student at Tanglewood in the summer of 1970. It was late in the evening — or, rather, early the next morning — and a group of us had been listening to favorite records in a dormitory room for several hours. Finally, about 2 A.M., a young pianist from Boston brought down an LP reissue of the "Mephisto Waltz." He told us, in brief, Kapell's story, put on the record with a knowing smile, and then watched our expressions as the manic, dizzying energy escaped once more from the grooves of the worn disc. It was our "nightcap;" nothing could have followed that experience.

The past few years have seen a revival of interest in Kapell's life and work. The Naumburg Foundation dedicated its 1979 International Competition to his memory; Peter Orth won first prize. In 1983, on the 30th anniversary of his death, "A Tribute to William Kapell" was presented at Symphony Space in Manhattan by the William Kapell Foundation for Contemporary Music and Musicians, founded by the pianist Michael Sellers. Many fine musicians — several of them Kapell colleagues — participated, and a brief kinescope of the pianist's 1953 appearance on the *Omnibus* television program was shown.

In 1985, the *Piano Quarterly* and the *New York Times* both published excerpts from Kapell's surviving diary. Since 1986, the Kapell archives have been housed at the International Piano Archives at the University of Maryland, which has reissued several recordings and issued others for the first time. The University of Maryland also sponsors the biannual International William Kapell Piano Competition. Radio announcers such as Claude Hermann, Piotr Kaminski, Phillippe Morin of France Musique and, in the United States, Leslie Gerber, Jim Sjveda and the present writer, among others, devoted programs (and sometimes whole series) to Kapell. WKCR-FM in New York presented

12 hours of recordings and interviews in 1987, in honor of what would have been Kapell's 65th birthday.

Kaminski entitled his series "A la recherche d'un pianiste perdu" — "In Search of a Lost Pianist." Alas, lost pianists cannot be found again. But the manifestations of Kapell's art and dedication survive, and they should be treasured by anybody who loves music.

19 ON AIRLINER DIE IN CRASH ON COAST

Craft From Australia Hits Peak Near San Francisco—Kapell, Noted Pianist, Is a Victim

Special to The New York Times.

SAN FRANCISCO, Oct. 29—A British Commonwealth Pacific Airlines plane crashed near here today, killing the nineteen persons on board.

The big DC-6, inbound from Australia, clipped a tree on a coastal ridge thirty-five miles southwest of this city, plowed into a mountainside and fell apart in flames.

William Kapell, 31 years old, New York pianist who was returning from a concert tour in Australia, was among the eleven passengers and eight crewmen losing their lives. Mr. Kapell was the only United States citizen in the plane. Most of the others were from Australia or the United Kingdom.

Many hours after the crash, which occurred at about 8:40 A. M. (11:40 A. M. Eastern standard time), members of search parties, who had difficulty getting through a dense woods at the base of King's Mountain, said that they could find no survivors.

Chief Petty Officer Wilson Jennings of the Coast Guard reported

Continued on Page 48, Column 3

The New York Times

OCTOBER 30, 1953.

KAPELL DISPLAYED HIS TALENT EARLY

Among Prizes Won by Pianist, Who Was Born in This City, Was Turkey Dinner With Iturbi

William Kapell was born here on Sept. 20, 1922, and showed musical talent at an early age. At 10, he began to study piano with Dorothea Anderson LaFollette at the Yorkville Settlement School.

Six weeks after taking his first lesson, the youth entered a contest open to students in city settlement schools and won first prize, a turkey dinner with José Iturbi, the pianist.

Mr. Kapell received his academic training at Columbia Grammar School, a private school in this city. During his senior year there, he received a scholarship to study under Mme. Olga Samaroff Stokowski at the Philadelphia Conservatory of Music.

Mr. Kapell won the 1940 Youth Contest of the Philadelphia Orchestra and made his debut with the orchestra in February, 1940, playing the Saint-Saëns G Minor Concerto.

In the fall of 1940 he received a Fellowship to the Juilliard Graduate School of Music. The following year he won the Walter W. Naumburg Musical Foundation competition and made his Town Hall debut as a Naumburg winner in October, 1941.

As a result of his Naumburg debut, Mr. Kapell received a second honor. In 1942 he was named winner of the Town Hall Endowment Series Award, given to the outstanding recitalist of the previous season under the age of 30. Mr. Kapell played his Endowment Series recital at Town Hall in February, 1942.

In the summer of 1942, he was chosen by Efrem Kurtz to introduce a new piano concerto by Aram Khachaturian with the Philharmonic-Symphony at Lewisohn Stadium. Mr. Kapell later played the concerto nearly thirty times with various orchestras in this country and abroad.

The pianist played his first concert tour in 1942 and thereafter made yearly tours of this country. His first tour abroad was in 1945.

PLANE CRASH VICTIM: William Kapell, concert pianist, who perished yesterday when a British Commonwealth Pacific airliner crashed and burned on the west coast after a flight from Australia and Honolulu.

when he went to Australia at the invitation of the Australian Broadcasting Commission. The following year he toured South America and in later seasons revisited Australia and made his first tours of Europe.

Mr. Kapell is survived by his parents, Mr. and Mrs. Harry Kapell; his wife, the former Rebecca Anna Lou Melson, and two children, David, 4 and Rebecca, 1.

'I Shall Never Return'

SYDNEY, Australia, Friday, Oct. 30 (UP)—Australian music lovers were deeply shocked today to learn of the death of Mr. Kapell. They were disturbed because he had ended his tour on a bitter note, charging he had been treated unfairly by the critics. His strangely prophetic parting remark was: "I shall never return. I mean what I say."

19 ON AIRLINER DIE IN CRASH ON COAST

Continued From Page 1

over a walkie-talkie that "it's a total strike" and "the only survivors here are in the rescue party."

The plane crashed soon after its commander, Capt. Bruce Dixon of Sydney, had reported at 8:39 A. M. by radio that he was over Half Moon Bay, a coastal town twenty miles southwest of the San Francisco International Airport.

He had been due at the airport almost an hour before, but he had reported no trouble, his fuel reserve was said to be ample, and he was coming in for a landing.

The ceiling at the airport was 1,200 feet, with visibility of ten miles. The highest point of King's Mountain, the crash scene, is 2,400 feet. The plane was above that height at the time of the control tower's last communication with Captain Dixon, and the pilot was instructed to come in, flying blind, on instruments.

An airport spokesman said that visibility was measured on the ground, and that even with a cloud ceiling of only a few hundred feet there sometimes was visibility of several miles. It was not unusual, he added, to order an instrument approach with a visibility of eight or ten miles and a ceiling of 1,200 feet, the conditions prevailing this morning.

Plane Wheels Believed Down

A preliminary investigation led to a tentative belief, based on the finding of a wheel near the spot where the craft first hit the mountainside, that Captain Dixon had his wheels down thinking he had cleared the King's Mountain ridges.

When the big plane failed to appear at the airport, ten miles south of here, the Coast Guard and the Air Force began rescue operations that led, nearly two hours later, to the sighting of the wreckage.

The ill-fated airliner was one of a fleet of DC-6's owned and operated by British Commonwealth Pacific Airlines, which, in turn, is jointly owned by the Australian, New Zealand and British Governments.

Captain Dixon had taken off last night from Honolulu on the last leg of the overwater trip of more than 8,000 miles from Sydney.

George Anderson, district traffic and sales manager for the company, said that the Australian Government was planning to buy the interests of the New Zealand and British Governments in the all-Australian airline. He added that this was the first accident for one of its planes.

SITE OF CRASH: Trans-Pacific plane struck a hill (cross) near San Francisco.

Mr. Bohlinger agreed that never

Continued on Page 14, Column 1

The Piano Player Had A Mind of His Own

By Paul Hume

THE plane carrying me safely to Los Angeles had barely landed when the shocking report of the death of William Kapell several hundred miles north came over the wires.

A profound feeling that this country, in young Kapell's death, lost one of its finest maturing artists was widely felt and expressed in every musical group I saw during a brief visit to California.

William Kapell

Kapell was only 31. For just over 10 years, he had worked, much harder than many who heard him may have realized, to make more encompassing the limits of his art. His debut appearances marked him as the leader in a young generation of pianists who had a phenomenal technical foundation.

As far as the notes went, there was nothing these brilliant youngsters could not play. The problem was whether or not they would be able to tap those subtlest resources of intellect and understanding that lead technicians into the realm of real art.

KAPELL could have been busy all his life, making a business career by playing the sensational piano concertos of Khatchaturian, Prokofieff, and Tschaikowsky, works in which his tremendous flair and prodigal abilities made him electric.

But at no time in his playing was this success his goal. It was fully five years ago that Kapell was engaged for his first solo recital in Washington. The program he submitted to the local manager was a model for a serious and, at the same time, virtuoso level of programing. He listed three sonatas, one each by Mozart, Brahms, and Aaron Copland, plus the great E Major Scherzo of Chopin, the last and greatest of the four, and the least played.

Kapell's New York manager called him into the office and said, "Willie, you aren't going to take this program out on the road for us." New York's big concert managements deny interfering with artists' programs, but this incident actually happened. And Kapell, declining to substitute the kind of program the New York boss thought the public would like, simply skipped his tour that year.

IN a long conversation last spring, Kapell told me about that season, and others, which led him to suggest to his management that perhaps they would never agree with him about the kind of music he wanted to play, and the way he wanted to make a career.

It was also last spring that Kapell talked about his immediate plans, which included playing accompaniments for a Schubert song recital during the summer of 1953, for an excellent Viennese soprano appearing at the Prades Festival directed by Pablo Casals. "This isn't the sort of thing people think I can or should do," Kapell said, "but it's one of the things I like to do most."

Reports from Prades rate his Schubert playing as some of the finest, most sensitive work heard in the entire summer there. Similarly, a recording of the massive Violin Sonata in D Minor, by Brahms, was made by Kapell and Heifetz. It was released close to the time of other recordings of the same work by Horowitz and Milstein, Isaac Stern and Zakin, Mischa Elman and Wolfgang Rose.

Kapell Was Living On Borrowed Time

SACRAMENTO (*P*) — A Sacramento pianist told yesterday how William Kapell, the brilliant young New York musician killed in the crash of a British airliner near San Francisco Thursday, once commented that he was living on "borrowed time."

Anthony Harris said Kapell visited him in May, 1952, after a concert here. Harris said he was aware of the intense schedule Kapell had mapped for himself and asked why he was driving himself so hard.

"I feel like I've got to do everything I can while there's time to do it; I've got cancer," Harris quoted Kapell. "The doctors have given me two years to live."

Two of the many critical tributes to Kapell published in the days after his death — Alexander Fried in the San Francisco *Examiner* and Paul Hume in the Washington *Post*. (Left) the Petaluma, California *Argus-Courier* fashioned this spurious item about a mythical cancer.

KAPELL DEATH MOURNED HERE

Brilliant Young Pianist Often Played in S. F.

By ALEXANDER FRIED.

The world of music — and particularly music in the United States — suffered a stunning blow yesterday in the death of William Kapell, young American pianist, who was aboard the British Commonwealth Pacific air liner that crashed on the Skyline Boulevard, towards the end of a trip to San Francisco from Australia.

Only thirty-one years old, married and the father of two small children, Kapell was frequently ranked as the most brilliant pianist this country ever pro-

WILLIAM KAPELL
Noted Pianist Killed
—Associated Press Wirephoto.

duced. Already often applauded here as symphony soloist, in solo recitals and chamber music, he was engaged to appear five times more with our orchestra this coming March.

In a typical review that I myself — thrilled at his keyboard genius — wrote of him little more than a year ago, I used the following words as lead:

"William Kapell — small, bushy-haired and all ajitter with an electric catlike nervous energy — played the piano like a young Horowitz and Rubinstein rolled into one, in Thursday night's San Francisco Symphony concert, conducted by Pierre Monteux, at the Opera House.

"His performance of Rachmaninoff's Third Concerto brought Horowitz to mind by its glowing surety and grandeur. And it had a Rubinstein quality of spontaneous flow and flourish."

It was part of Kapell's genius that he was so studious and individual in his playing. His touch was beautiful. His poetic spirit ran deep. He had a temperament that could whip up the keyboard to tempestuous climax.

Born in New York, Kapell never was the type of musician who suffered for lack of recognition. At the age of only 20, he became the youngest person ever to win the all-important Town Hall Endowment Series Award. The victory gained him eminent sponsorship in a prize New York solo recital.

In the same year, 1942, he was already soloist with the New York Philharmonic-Symphony. Soon he was touring the United States time and again, from coast to coast. He played abroad in Australia, South America, Europe and Israel. His March concerts with the San Francisco Symphony — at the Opera House, in the Standard radio series and in Fresno — were to have presented him under the guest conductorship of Enrique Jorda.

Kapell's wife — Anna Lou Nelson, of Portland, Ore. — also was a pianist until they married in 1948. They met when she was studying in Chicago, he gave a concert there and after the concert she went backstage to compliment him. Their two children are Rebecca, aged 2, and David, aged 5.

Until several weeks ago, Mrs. Kapell was with her famous husband on his Australian tour. Then she flew back by herself to her home in New York. It is said that during his trip home, Kapell intended at first to stop off in Honolulu. He changed his mind for some reason, and remained aboard the plane. This decision brought about the crashing fatal chord that ended an ever great and always growing musical career.

MUSIC AND MUSICIANS
By VIRGIL THOMSON

Kapell

THE pianist William Kapell, who died in an airplane accident near San Francisco on Oct. 29, was a great artist. So were Grace Moore, soprano; Ginette Neveu and Jacques Thibaud, violinists, who have died in similar fashion in recent years. Every time an airplane falls persons distinguished in professional, political, business or military life are among the dead. Because, it is exactly such persons to whom the speed of air travel offers an irresistible convenience. A musician who moves about the globe in this way can play twice to three times as many engagements a season as the one who is earthbound. Also it is known that aviation fatalities per passenger-mile traveled are far fewer than those due to the deadly automobile. Still, the number of famous names that appears in the aviation accident lists is impressive. And still the advantages, economic and artistic, that come from being able to move quickly from one date to another will keep a large number of our most valued musicians among the inveterate air travelers.

First Decade

AMONG musicians of his generation William Kapell, just thirty-one on Sept. 20, was one of the great ones. His career, like that of Ginette Neveu, was at the point where he was no longer considered a mere boy genius but was recognized by his colleagues as a mature artist. At nineteen he was winning big prizes. At twenty he began his career as a touring recitalist and a much-in-demand orchestral soloist. But for a decade his repertory had remained heavily weighted with the easy-to-put-over works of Rachmaninoff, Tchaikovsky and Khatchaturian. It was only in the last two years that he had gained real access to the grand repertory of the piano, to the concertos of Mozart and Beethoven and Brahms and Chopin and to the suites of Bach and Debussy, and that he had been genuinely successful with that repertory.

Maturity

KAPELL had fought hard for this access and for this success. He had fought with his management and with the press. And he had wrestled with the repertory itself, not only alone but also with the counsel and the detailed co-operation of musicians who knew that repertory. He had studied, labored, consulted, digested, grown. Kapell had become a grown man and a mature artist, a master. He could play great music with authority; his readings of it were at once musically sound and genuinely individual. He had a piano technique of the first class, a powerful mind, a consecration and a working ability such as are granted to few, and the highest aspirations toward artistic achievement.

Conquest

KAPELL was conquering the world. In one decade he had won a world-wide audience. At the beginning of a second he was recognized as a master to be taken seriously in the great piano repertory. He was already laying plans (and operating, too) toward the renewal of the repertory through the application of his great technical and interpretative powers to contemporary piano music and through devoted co-operation with contemporary composers. And his conquests were not easy. Few artists have ever battled so manfully with management or so unhesitatingly sassed the press. He was afraid of nobody, because his heart was pure.

Bright Star, Dark Star

IT IS not germane that as a man he was a good son and brother, a good husband and father and a loyal friend, though he was all these. What is important to music is that he was a great musician and a great fighter. He did not fight for himself or for just any music. He fought to play well and to play the best music. Also to take part in the creative life of his time. And he was winning, would have gone on winning, for he had a star.

He also had an unlucky star, else he would not have been taken from us. And our loss, music's loss, is irreparable. Other men of comparable genius and sincerity may arise; but none will ever take his place, because that place was unique. Kapell had built it to fit his own great talents. And built it so that his talents could serve the whole world of music in their own particular and powerful way. Past services will remain and be of use to others. But Kapell himself, that huge life-force, is dead; and his continuing musical presence will not be with us any more. Since he was buried last Monday it has been a week of mourning for musicians.

Kapell's Death Loss To Music
By LOUIS BIANCOLLI.

It was my friend and associate, Bob Bagar, in the midst of a music critics' reunion at the Lotos Club, who told me last week that William Kapell was dead. I have rarely been so stunned by news of tragedy.

There was everything ahead for the boy—his biggest concert season, a huge recording schedule, mounting recognition from all sides. This was all small, no doubt, beside the fact that he left behind him an adoring wife and two children and a mother and father who worshipped him. That, after all, is the real horror.

I knew Kapell slightly—a few words in the lobby of Carnegie Hall, a cordial hello on the street, a wave of the hand from the top of the stairs at Carnegie Hall. My most lingering vision of him off-stage was of the dapper little fellow coming down those stairs with his lovely wife. I shall treasure that moment.

Into Magic Realm.

Otherwise, I knew Kapell only as the slender and serious-looking youth who walked out on the stage of Carnegie Hall to take his place at the piano for another flight into the magic realm of music. Kapell loved the piano, loved his music, and loved the people he played to. He was a born artist.

There had been struggle in his life—struggle and self-denial and an endless striving toward higher and higher levels of perfection. At 31 he had attained a remarkably secure and enviable place in the musical scheme of things; and at 31 he was abruptly, cruelly, needlessly cut off from it all.

Kapell had gone through periods of sharp self-examination when he had cause to wonder whether he was, after all, on the right track. There was this almost unparalleled technique of his, this whirlwind virtuosity that swept through the most gruelling music with astonishing facility.

A Greater Artist.

I believe at one point he feared it might be controlling him, instead of the other way around. But he applied himself afresh, restudied the whole mechanism of interpretation and came back a greater artist.

This prodigious gift Kapell had very early—long before he went to the late Olga Samaroff-Stokowski. One has only to hear a recording made of two movements of Beethoven's C minor concerto, while he was studying with Dorothea LaFollette, to realize what a poet and virtuoso he already was at 14.

Chicago Daily
Today with Women
MOVIES • AMUSEMENTS

F Part 2—Page 1

Friday, October 30, 1953

On the Aisle
In Memory of William Kapell, Who Left Us Richer in Music

BY CLAUDIA CASSIDY

NO ONE will deny the loss to music that was the sudden, violent, pitifully shocking death of William Kapell, just 31, killed in a plane crash on the homecoming lap of a long and exhausting Australian tour. To those who valued him as a pianist, the loss will be one of degree; to those who loved him as pianist and friend, it is irreparable.

When I say as pianist and friend, the words fall in that order by natural sequence. Willy was a pianist first, last and always. You had to understand that. There was in him the relentless, terrible and wonderful compulsion of genius. He had to play. He had to play better than anyone else in the world. This was not vanity. It was nothing so cheap, so ephemeral, so unworthy. It was an ever deepening sense of responsibility. It was humility in the face of music.

When I first heard him at Ravinia in 1943, he was 20, catapulted to fame by the Khachaturian Concerto he was playing. It was not much of a concerto, but no one else has played it like that, with beauty and sweep and fire. It served notice, that concerto, of what was to come. Perhaps it was only just that it came, in a flood of splendor, at that same Ravinia in the summer of 1947. He played the Third Rachmaninoff Concerto, which he was to have played this New Year's eve with Fritz Reiner and the Chicago Symphony orchestra in Orchestra hall.

No one who heard it will forget that performance. With it Kapell moved into the company of Horowitz and Rachmaninoff himself, who alone had conquered the citadel of that strange concerto, which is cheap unless it is magnificent. He forged the full splendor of the score from his amazing equipment of poetry and fire, of impishness and blazing technique. He conjured its curious fragrance by coaxing from the piano its loveliest songs.

From then on it was to me just a question of time when Kapell would be the foremost pianist. Season after season, that time came closer. He played crystalline Mozart, a Bach suite of unforgettable purity of tone. His Brahms rose from the deepest lyricism, yet knew the inimical and the brusque. It poured out in a torrent of fabulous performance last season in the most extraordinary performance I have known of the D Minor Concerto. I called that playing fabulous. The word stands.

These were performances the world knew. Some of the most beautiful only his friends shared. He was not ready to give them to the public. He would come to our house late at night, after relentless hours of the slavery that is practice, and he would listen to a few records. To Caruso, for that prodigal outpouring of glorious tone. To Schnabel, whom he adored. To the quality of Rachmaninoff the pianist, of Horowitz the technical wizard. Serkin's Beethoven, the voluminous Rubenstein tone. But the piano always recaptured and held him, whatever the hour, and the neighbors never complained. Perhaps they knew their luck. For they heard Schubert, Schumann, Beethoven, the music of Spain, the Bach to come—they heard what is now unbelievably, no more.

It is not easy to be such a pianist. It means slavery, sacrifice. It means in the concert hall to open your heart so wide you are incredibly vulnerable. He was, this smouldering, passionate, young pianist, generous, lovable, deeply gentle of heart. I loved his playing above all other playing, and this can scarcely be a secret to anyone who has read this column. So not for myself, but to tell you what he was like, now that he is gone, here is a part of one of his last letters:

"Why do you think playing in Chicago always is some sort of test for me? Because I know there is one incredible woman whose heart can't be misled. So, neither is mine. And God alone realizes how creatures such as I need you to inspire them with an unwavering standard. Music isn't enough. Performers aren't enough. There must be someone who loves music as much as life. For you, and remember this always, those of us with something urgent to say, we give everything."

Kapell gave, and I am eternally grateful that I was here to

"I Shall Never Return"

Manhattan-born William Kapell was a hammer-handed but unmistakably talented pianist of 19 when he first crashed onto the U.S. music scene in a concert with the Philadelphia Orchestra in 1941. In rapid order, he won three important awards, gathered a devoted following and dazzled the critics with his performances. "Playing of Rachmaninoff dimensions," cheered the *Times's* Olin Downes. "Complete mastery, with prodigious strength and swiftness." Kapell appeared with 20 major orchestras, and his bouncing plume of black hair became familiar to concert audiences across the U.S.

As time passed, the critics developed a more exacting tone. Kapell's real forte, they ruled, was the moderns, e.g., his favorite Prokofiev and Khachaturian, and such technically demanding romantics as Rachmaninoff. With other music, they sometimes complained, he lacked "tonal sensuousness." But without hesitation, they placed him among the top young pianists of his time. Pianist Kapell looked for new fields to conquer, took himself as far afield as Europe, South America, Israel, Australia.

Fortnight ago, ending his second tour of Australia, he sounded a bitter note. Riffling through his press notices, he read that though his Schubert had "surprising warmth," his Mozart was merely "well-bred," his Bach "dry."

"Dry Bach!" he exclaimed to a reporter for Sydney's *Sunday Telegraph*. "Listen to this." And the room, wrote the reporter, "was filled with liquid sound, mellow, golden," as Kapell turned to his keyboard. But Kapell had his fill of Sydney critics; it was goodbye forever. "I shall never return," he said.

Last week Pianist Kapell, 31, took off in a British Commonwealth Pacific Airlines DC-6 for the long flight home. Eight thousand miles later, letting down for an instrument landing at San Francisco, the big ship clipped a fog-concealed tree, crashed headlong into the side of a mountain ravine. Among the 19 who died in the flames was William Kapell.

Thomson, Cassidy and Biancolli weighed in with solemn tributes to Kapell; *Time* emphasized the irony of the pianist's last interview.

EUGENE ORMANDY
THE BELLEVUE-STRATFORD
PHILADELPHIA 2, PENNSYLVANIA

November 5 - 1953.

Dearest Annalou,

On Monday, on our return home, I told the Orchestra of Willy's and your love for them.

That evening we played the "Eroica" Symphony, and before we began I told the audience of the irreparable loss the music world has suffered and of our love for Willy, and of his for us, and concluded with these words: "The members of the Philadelphia Orchestra and I would like to play the Funeral March movement in memory of our departed friend." We did.

Write us, dearest Annalou, if there is anything we can do for you.

Our love - always, Eugene.

Eugene Ormandy, perhaps Kapell's most ardent champion among conductors, was one of the many musicians who sent letters of consolation to Anna Lou. (Right) Aaron Copland published his eulogy in the *Saturday Review*.

The Measure of Kapell

DEAR ANNA LOU: When a dear friend is lost to us we try to bring some solace to the nearest of kin by writing a letter. Many thousands of music lovers in many parts of the world must have felt that impulse when they learned of your husband's tragic end on October 29. I too had that impulse, and writing you this letter my hope is that I may possibly express some of the things that are certainly in the hearts of William Kapell's many admirers.

When I think of Willie I think of him as having been above all else the personification of the artist. Except for yourself and the children, I never recall discussing anything but music with him. The singleness of his passion for the art we both loved was almost frightening, even to a composer like myself. It was as if the sound of music created an hypnotic spell about him—and whether it was sound made by himself or sound listened to made little essential difference. When music was heard nothing else mattered. I know that this is said to be true for most musicians, but for the most part that is a pleasant fiction; in Willie's case it was quite literally true. As you well know, to him a house without a piano was no better than an empty shell; to find himself in a situation where no piano was within easy reach was physically intolerable. In that connection he more than once reminded me of George Gershwin—seeing either of them in a room where there was a piano meant that sooner or later the man and the instrument would meet.

All this has little significance compared with the way in which William was profoundly the artist, both in his very nature and in the symbolic role he was fated to play in the concert world. The artist in him was startlingly evident in his person and in his performing gift: he was passionate, intense, restless, devoted, in love with perfection as a goal, forever striving toward that goal—straining toward it, even. At times his friends must have seemed inadequate and distant to him, for the force and drive of his temperament were such as necessarily to make him dissatisfied when confronted with the signs of sweet reasonableness. His questioning and demanding spirit gave off sparks of a youthfulness that never left him. Willie, if he had lived, would always have remained a youthful artist, in the best sense of that term. The search for artistic growth, the ideal of maturity was a central and continuing preoccupation with him. Emerson once wrote that the artist is "pitiful." He meant, I suppose, that the true artist can never be entirely satisfied with the work he does. William Kapell was that kind of true artist.

And yet he was among the few top pianists of our time. Why? What qualities were particularly his? There were brilliance and drama in his playing, songfulness and excitement. On the platform he had the fire and abandon that alone can arouse audiences to fever pitch. He knew his power, and I have no doubt was sometimes frightened by it. The big public can be a potential menace, after all; it can elicit the best and the worst from the artist. Characteristically, when playing on the stage, Willie often turned his head away from the auditorium, the better to forget us I imagine. Nevertheless, even when most lost within himself, he instinctively projected his playing into the hall, for he was indubitably the performer. I cannot conceive of his ever having given a dull performance—an erratic one perhaps, a misguided or stylistically incongruous one maybe, but invariably one that was electric and alive.

We both know that he was, at times, an easy target for the reviewers of the daily press. He exaggerated their importance, ignored the good things said, and remembered only the bad. I always took this to be a measure of his own seriousness. The successful performer of today cannot plead ignorance of his own playing. He has the recorded disc for mirror. Willie knew better than anyone when he was in top form; to be unjustly evaluated after such performances pained and tortured him. Unlike the composer in a similar position, he could not expect justification from posterity. No wonder he was unusually nervous before stepping on the platform. Like every basically romantic artist, he never could predict what was about to happen on the stage, but on the other hand the satisfaction of an outstanding performance must have been enormous.

I shall always treasure the thought of William's deep attachment to my own music. He never tired of telling

Kapell—"personification of the artist."

me what my music meant to him; and I, on my part, never ceased being surprised at the intensity of his feeling for it. What was most surprising was his fondness for the most forbidding aspects of my music; he repeatedly played precisely those pieces that his audiences were least likely to fathom. He played them with a verve and grandeur and authority that only a front-rank pianist is able to bring to unfamiliar music. He played them, I often felt, in a spirit of defiance: defiance of managers with their cautious notions of what was right and fitting for a Kapell program; defiance of the audience that had come to hear him in works from the regular repertoire; played them, one might almost say, in defiance of his own best interests. In actuality I believe he played them in order to satisfy a deep need—the need every artist has to make connection with the music of his own time. I am touched and moved at the thought of the high regard in which he held them. His programming of new music was an act of faith; it was Willie's contribution toward a solution of one of the most disturbing factors in our musical life: namely, the loss of connection between the performer and the contemporary composer of his own time.

When William died he was expecting a new piano work from my pen. It was a promise I had gladly given him. It is a promise I intend to keep, and when the work is written I can only hope that it will be worthy of the best in William Kapell.

My love and sympathy are with you.
—AARON COPLAND.

WILLIAM KAPELL (1922-1953)

On October 29th, 1953, William Kapell died in an air accident returning to the United States from a tour in Australia. The world of music had lost one of its great artists tragically early in his life and his career.

He first appeared on the musical scene in 1942. In the eleven short years that followed he conquered the world by the beauty and perfection of his piano playing and toward the end by the depth of his art.

I loved William Kapell as a loyal friend and admired him as an artist above all others in his generation.

He participated in these concerts last summer playing the Mozart Concerto K 453 with the orchestra under Maître Casals as well as Schubert Lieder with Maria Stader, a Beethoven Sonata with Arthur Grumiaux and a Mozart Piano Quartet with Grumiaux, Milton Thomas and Paul Tortelier.

His visit here will always be one of the most precious souvenirs of these Festivals.

EUGENE ISTOMIN.

Eugene Istomin's tribute to his friend and colleague, published in the Prades Festival's program booklet the summer after Kapell's death.

Kapell did not live to play this duo recital with Joseph Schuster, scheduled for the spring of 1954 in Los Angeles.

Copland created his most
ambitious keyboard work,
the vast Piano Fantasy,
in memory of Kapell.

> Commissioned by the Juilliard School of Music,
> William Schuman, President,
> on the occasion of its fiftieth anniversary celebration
>
> and
>
> Dedicated to the memory of
> William Kapell

PROGRAM NO

Aaron Copl
School of Music
completed on Ja
William Kapell.

Mr. Copland

"Sketches fo
the composer's no
work on the Fanta
France, at the M
poser's home in t
extended works f
Piano Sonata (19
absolute music. It
materials. The co
would suggest the
premeditated sequ
possible) from th
emplifying clear

"The musica
sequence of ten d
joined, subsequentl
out as a kind of
are elements able
with music tonall
rigorously controll
of devices associat

ıtasy was commissioned by J
ı of its fiftieth anniversary ar
. It is dedicated to the mem

:he following note on the work:

piano solo work are to be fo
back as the early fifties. Cons
on during 1955 and 1956 in Sc
y in New Hampshire and at th
ley. Like the composer's two p
the Piano Variations (1930) a
v Fantasy belongs in the categ
whatever of folk or popular r
se was to attempt a compositio
ıtasy, that is, a spontaneous a
s' that would carry the listen
the last, while at the same ti
ınconventional structural princi

of the entire piece is based u
of the chromatic scale. To the
ed tones of the scale, treated th
val. Thus inherent in the ma
ed with the twelve tone method and
'he Piano Fantasy is by no means
music, but it does make liberal use
echnique."

PROGRAM
SEASON 1957-58

Juilliard School of Music

presents

The World Premiere of

Piano Fantasy

Aaron Copland

(1955-57)

Friday evening, October 25, 1957 at 8:30
Juilliard Concert Hall
130 Claremont Avenue, New York City

William Masselos, *pianist*

RADIO CORPORATION OF AMERICA
RCA VICTOR RECORD DIVISION
155 E. 24TH STREET
NEW YORK 10, N.Y.

MU9-7200

December 12, 1960

Mrs. Anna Lou deHavenon
1150 Fifth Avenue
New York, N.Y.

Dear Anna Lou:

I have had a check made of the entire catalog, and am reluctantly confirming that all of Willie's records are now catalog cut-outs, the most recent ones having been deleted only this year. They include the following:

64
32 mm
4 track
single track
spool —

LM-1715	Chopin Sonata and Mazurkas
LM-1791	Bach-Schubert-Liszt
LM-1865	Chopin Mazurkas
LM-9026	Beethoven No. 2 and Rachamninoff Rhapsody

The others were cut out last year, and they include:

LM-1006	Khatchaturian Concerto
LVT-1028	Prokofieff Concerto No. 3
LM-1097	Rachmaninoff Concerto No. 2

There are some unreleased recordings in the ice-box which Willie never approved, but we are currently discussing a reissue program and I hope to have more information about this shortly. We have found that the Camden reissues at a lower price have a relatively short life in the catalog, and after discussing this with some of my colleagues, I am of the opinion that this might not be the best approach.

RCA Pioneered and Developed Compatible Color Television
RCA VICTOR RECORDS

The problem of getting t
a substantial one, and I
of the two most likely s
Record Collectors Exchang
the other being Merit Mus
They charge a premium, of
would be the best source

I will expect to hear fro
material that you have. A
would be for us to have ta
that are now cut out, but
I should think $150 or $20
want this done, I am sure

All best.

Sincerely,

Alan Kayes
Manager
Red Seal Artists & Repertoir

NATIONAL AFFAIRS

DEFENSE:
Move to Unify

On the surface, the Pentagon announcement last week that the Air Force will be the single agency for all military space development seemed plain enough. Secretary of Defense Robert S. McNamara simply explained that, to avoid duplication and save money, it was best to put the Pentagon's space eggs in one basket. Under certain "unusual circumstances" to be decided by himself, McNamara said, the Army and Navy may occasionally be allowed to dabble in space ventures, and they can keep the major programs they now have. But to all intents and purposes the Pentagon's three-pronged space effort was now over; the Army and Navy would have to take a back seat to the Air Force.

Yet if this was the surface meaning of McNamara's announcement, to Pentagon insiders there was a good deal more that did not meet the eye.

In reality, Mr. Kennedy—through McNamara—was making his first big move toward eventual unification of the services. And he was doing it in a wholly unlooked-for way. NEWSWEEK's Lloyd Norman reported:

The truth is that the President is shelving Stuart Symington's traditionshattering recommendation for a single chief of staff at the head of a unified military force. This is simply something that would generate too much opposition on Capitol Hill. Instead, Mr. Kennedy is boldly proposing to achieve unification on his own—by Executive decree, if necessary, or just such orders from McNamara as the space-control decision. The ultimate goal: A single command tightly controlled by the President and the Defense Secretary themselves.

As McNamara's planners cautiously join the trend, the Joint Chiefs of [Staff] remain in nominal control of [operations]. But they will [eventually] be limited to re-[porting], and supplying the op-[tions] needed.

Computers: Of necessity, [McNamara]'s new approach will be a [rev]olutionary process rather [than an ove]rnight reshaping of the Pen-[tagon. Ins]iders expect that tough ex-[ecutive] McNamara will lean more and [more on] his civilian advisers (the Air [Force, for] example, was recom-[mended mo]ve, by his new office for Organiza-[tion a]nd Management Planning, headed [by Ha]rvard-trained lawyer Sol Horwitz). [Alrea]dy McNamara is adapting stream-[lined] industrial techniques to military [pla]nning (one: the use of electronic [c]omputers to weigh the cost of

March 20, 1961

competing weapons systems).

There could yet be many a snag in Mr. Kennedy's plans, for interservice jealousy dies hard. At the weekend, Gen. Lyman Lemnitzer, chairman of the Joint Chiefs (and an Army man), already was protesting that McNamara's space order went "too far." But there were also old-timers at the Pentagon willing to bet that it could be brought off—that the inevitable trend is toward unification. As one put it: "It now looks for the first time as if we are going to have a single Department of Defense —not a bunch of competing services."

AIRLINES:
An Artist's Life

In the Federal District Court in New York this week there will open a precedent-making trial at the heart of which is this question: Exactly how much is the life of an artist worth?

The artist was William Kapell, a slight and shock-haired young pianist who—had he lived—might have become one of the world's most famous performers. But Kapell, born in near-poverty in a room above a New York City bookstore, and acclaimed a genius at the age of 19, was killed in 1953. He died in the crash of an airliner near San Francisco.

Kapell, then 31 and the father of two young children, was the best-known of nineteen persons who perished when a DC-6B, near the end of a flight from Australia, brushed against a tree and plunged into a ravine. So far as British Commonwealth Pacific Airlines (a corporate ancestor of Qantas) was concerned, whatever Kapell's worth as an artist, Kapell's life was worth $8,000 to his widow, Rebecca. That's the limit that the 80-odd airlines belonging to IATA (International Air Transport Association) have agreed to pay in any case of personal injury on an international flight where the airline is not plainly at fault.

Despite the limit, Kapell's widow and children are suing this week for $1 million damages. To pursue the claim they have hired a San Francisco lawyer named Melvin Belli, whose reputation for winning personal-injury cases (NEWS-WEEK, July 18) has won him the title of "King of Torts."*

Belli delayed bringing the suit these

*Literally, twistings. In law those wrongs not covered by contract on which civil suits can be based.

Kapell: $8,000 or $500,000 for genius?

seven years for a good reason. He wanted first to try another case arising from the same crash, the death of refugee Hungarian law student Janos Fehrer and his young son. Before the same judge who will hear the Kapell case, District Judge Willis W. Ritter, Belli established that the DC-6B's pilot had been reckless, collected $35,000 damages for the Fehrer estate. Then he was ready to take on the Kapell case.

In trying to prove his claims in the Kapell case, Belli will play Kapell's phonograph records in court and he will call on such musical notables as conductor Leonard Bernstein, pianist José Iturbi, and violinist Jascha Heifetz. Their purpose, of course, will be to testify to the artistic stature of Kapell and to assess, if only in financial terms, the value of the artist's life.

CALIFORNIA:
Dreadful Dilemma

Only hours before he was to die in the gas chamber of San Quentin prison for the holdup slaying of a Los Angeles policeman, Erwin (Machine Gun) Walker went gibbering mad—and so could not be executed under California statutes. That was back in 1949.

This week, some twelve years and $30,000 worth of psychotherapy later, the threat of the gas chamber hung over Walker once again. A judge had ac-

29

The 1960s: All recordings
out of print; a lawsuit
pursued, won, and after
fifteen years, finally
overturned.

The late 1970s saw a resurgence of interest in Kapell's work. (Below) Anna Lou and Van Cliburn with Peter Orth, immediately after the young pianist won the 1979 Naumberg Competition dedicated to Kapell's memory. (Right) In the fall of 1983, a Kapell memorial program was presented on the Upper West Side of Manhattan.

IN MEMORY OF
WILLIAM KAPELL
(September 20, 1922 - October 29, 1953)

featuring pianists:

**DICKRAN ATAMIAN
LUKAS FOSS
RICHARD GOODE
GARY GRAFFMAN
JEROME LOWENTHAL
WILLIAM MASSELOS
SHIRLEY RHOADS
MICHAEL SELLERS**

performing works by

CHOPIN, LISZT, MENDELSSOHN, SCRIABIN, SCHUBERT, SAMUEL BARBER, AARON COPLAND, LUKAS FOSS, GEORGE PERLE, and the world premiere of *Toccata* by RICHARD CAMERON-WOLFE.

WEDNESDAY EVENING, OCTOBER 26, 1983 at 8:0
The Symphony Space - 95th Street and Broadway

Tickets: $25 Benefactors' Contribution for concert plus reception;
$8 General Admission to Concert.
TDF + $4, subject to availability. See other side for details and order form.

Reflections on William Kapell on the 30th Anniversary of His Death

Dear Willy:

We're all here tonight to praise you, celebrate you, and mourn you. You always had praise, and understood it for what it was, and you were used to being celebrated. Being mourned is something else again: yet you were acquainted with that too. You spent so much of your abrupt life mourning your own daily deaths, grieving over what you perceived to be your failures, even as you celebrated your own flaming genius. I still see you clawing at yourself in a furious despair; exactly as David mourning Jonathan rent his garments, and Job and Jeremiah theirs, so you would rend the fleshly garment of your body, prophesying your own tragedy.

Now, again, we mourn with you the tragedy that you were never permitted to be old, just as you had never enjoyed being young. There was no time for either youth or age: only the few years for the fierce celebration of the Eucharist you knew as music.

You remember our talking about Auden in 1946? I read you the poem that begins:

> *About suffering they were never wrong,*
> *The Old Masters...*

More than any artist I've ever known, you understood that line.

OCTOBER 14, 1983   LEONARD BERNSTEIN

In his short life William Kapell conquered the world with his beautiful piano playing. He left the highest standard ever achieved by an American born pianist.

His intensity, his translucent sound, his humble yet steely discipline and piercing intelligence, above all his powerful personality combined with a sometimes feisty integrity, describe him best as an artist and force of nature.

Are four or five seasons of superlative playing enough to enshrine him in the Pantheon? I don't know—we hardly had time to realize and he was gone—so that even now, thirty years later I remain incredulous and unconsolable. Of course we continue, but are diminished by the abortion of his career.

He died so unfinished as to make mockery of the purpose of his marvelous gifts. Yet to me he is still undimmed and very very close, ever formidable, ever a spur to my conscience to justify the purpose of my own.

October 12, 1983   EUGENE ISTOMIN

From the booklet distributed at the Symphony Space concert.

from the performers in tonight's concert:

When I first heard William Kapell on record, in 1980, I felt that up until then I had been cheated: that my ears had been cheated of hearing one of the truly wondrous talents that had ever come before the public. His euphoric, melodic playing combined with that demonic drive was almost too much for one listener to comprehend, it seemed. But I listened and listened until I had heard everything he'd ever recorded in concert or in the studio. It was the most moving music-making that I had ever encountered. There was a sense of regret at missing what he must have been to see and hear onstage, but also a sense of contentment in just hearing the sound he made with his instrument: it was all one, as if Kapell was the piano and the piano him. This was what piano playing surely must be all about, and I have never since stopped wondering at how much pleasure he must have given to both himself and his audience.

DICKRAN ATAMIAN

I never heard William Kapell in concert, but I remember the powerful impression I received when a friend played for me his recording of the Bach *D Major Partita*. The purity, strength, and boldness of that playing which seemed to come from such a deep source, will always be an inspiration to musicians.

RICHARD GOODE

William Kapell was undoubtedly the most important pianist of his generation. Thirty years later he still haunts me with his fiercely uncompromising standards. He set an impeccable and unforgettable musical example.

GARY GRAFFMAN

To me, William Kapell was like the very flame of art. He taught me music with the same generosity, the same intensity of commitment, and the same range and focus of vision as those which distinguished his playing. My three years of study with him were illumined by a sense of privilege which time has only ripened.

JEROME LOWENTHAL

Though Willy was almost my brother at Juilliard, the memory of him has faded in the 40 years since—faded, except for two things that always stay fresh, two flowers that cannot die. Here is Willy, wearing a wool shirt that gives him a rash: scratching both arms with both hands, he laughs and says, "I'm on fire!" And here he is on the corner of 43rd and Broadway. For some reason or other, the word "enigma" has fascinated him; he says "enigma" over and over again, now loud, now soft, but always with gaiety and concentration.

There is a third, indelible memory; it is Willy in '51 or '52 playing the Copland *Variations* with such a punch that it makes me feel ill. "If I ever learn another Copland," I say to myself, "this will be the one." And so, indeed, it was: I was to play the *Variations* often—Willy's gift, his enigma, his fire.

WILLIAM MASSELOS

In the last three years of his life William Kapell became my friend and mentor. I was a young pianist living in Chicago. He was there often on his way to and from concerts. I would play for him and listen to him play. We went to concerts and talked about music and life, in that order, over steaks ("rare and *no parsley*") at the Blackstone Hotel, where he often stayed. His intensity of purpose, some would say his obsession, to make his playing as beautiful as possible, for *music's* sake, extended to his friends and colleagues, in the demands he made upon them, and in his expectations. He would suggest or exhort, depending on the circumstances. He would go to any source to learn something and was impatient with the pride and arrogance that could prevent a musician from learning more about music and its performance, no matter where he was in his career, if it needed to be learned. He took and he gave with integrity, generosity, humor, and a sense of what life was all about.

SHIRLEY RHOADS

William Kapell has been one of my pianistic "patron saints" since boyhood. For my thirteenth Christmas I had asked for a phonograph, and a month or so beforehand, confident that I would receive one, I took money I had saved and bought my first recording: Kapell's "Second Rachmaninoff Concerto."

Subsequently I acquired all of his other RCA recordings, and I would listen to them by the hour. As I grew more sophisticated musically I became increasingly aware of the very special qualities in his playing: a dazzling brilliance, an electric rhythm, a galvanizing sweep and drive, an iridescent beauty and fullness of tone, an awareness of styles, a comprehensive musicianship, and an awesome honesty and integrity. All of these qualities were fused with an inner fire and intensity that inspired me to become a pianist.

One of the great wishes of my life is that I could have known Willy or have heard him play in person. Nevertheless, through the years I have strongly felt his influence and presence in my life.

On the wall near my piano is a photo of Willy practicing which could be entitled "Work Is Sacred." It personifies for me what it means to be an artist: striving, idealistic, noble, visionary.

MICHAEL SELLERS

Honoring the memory of a legendary pianist

Recalling a pianist of legend

By Daniel Webster
Inquirer Music Critic

NEW YORK — If America has a legendary pianist, it is William Kapell. Since his death at age 31 in a fiery plane crash near San Francisco, his playing, his personality and his image have been raised to something of a myth by performers, critics, friends and composers.

The memory is particularly vivid in Philadelphia, where the young pianist studied and played his first orchestral concerts.

Last night, exactly 30 years after Kapell's death in 1953, some of his admirers met to perform music ranging from Schubert to Aaron Copland as a means of clarifying their view of his fiery life and art. Chief among the performers was Chicago-born pianist Michael Sellers, who two years ago founded the William Kapell Piano Foundation, sponsor of the memorial concert. Other performers included Gary Graffman, Richard Goode, Dickran Atamian, William Masselos, Lukas Foss, Sellers and Jerome Lowenthal, Kapell's pupil from Philadelphia.

All of the players profess near-worship of Kapell, and each chose works that could demonstrate their homage.

The concert, held at Symphony Space on Manhattan's Upper West Side, included the premiere of Richard Cameron-Wolfe's Toccata, commissioned for the event, and a performance of Copland's Piano Fantasy, written for Kapell but premiered after his death by Masselos.

Although a New Yorker by birth, the young Kapell was adopted by Philadelphians during the time he studied at the Philadelphia Conservatory with the pianist Olga Samaroff Stokowski. In 1940, at 18, he made his orchestral debut as a winner of the Philadelphia Orchestra's youth auditions. Frederic R. Mann, the paper-box manufacturer and philanthropist, became Kapell's patron and paid for his training. When Kapell was only 22, Eugene Ormandy took the unprecedented step of signing Kapell to a contract guaranteeing annual performances and recordings with the Philadelphia Orchestra.

Kapell launched an international career with that support, playing the late romantic showpieces and works he commissioned from Copland, Vil-

(See KAPELL on 5-E)

KAPELL, from 1-E

la-Lobos and many others. His death shocked the country, for Kapell already was recognized as an American export equal to any European master.

In Saturday Review magazine, Copland published a letter to Kapell's widow, Anna Lou, that tried to measure Kapell's stature.

"Kapell's questioning and demanding spirit gave off sparks of a youthfulness that never left him," wrote Copland in the letter, which has become a classic. "Willie, if he had lived, would have remained a youthful artist."

Of Kapell's performances of his music, Copland wrote, "I never ceased being surprised at the intensity of his feeling for it.... He repeatedly played those pieces that his audiences were least likely to fathom. He played them with a verve and grandeur and authority that only a front-rank pianist is able to bring to unfamiliar music.

"He played them, one might almost say, in defiance of his own best interests.... He played them in order to satisfy a deep need — the need every artist has to make connection with the music of his own time."

In the memorial concert, Kapell is seen as the icon of musicians who feel performers and composers live isolated from each other.

"When Kapell died, he had negotiated a contract for a European tour which insisted that one American work be included in every concert he played," Sellers said before the concert. "When I established this foundation, it was because I'd like to see more composers get interested in the piano. You see George Rochberg or George Crumb write a couple of pieces but not a lot of pieces. The piano is not a favorite today, and that leads to neglect in the development of the literature.

"I'd like to see performers have more contact with composers," he went on, "and I'd like to see the development of audience interest. I think an audience should hear new music integrated with standard works to stimulate their interest and perspective. That was Kapell's way."

Sellers said Kapell was an idol of his even before he decided to become a musician.

"Kapell was already dead when I heard his recording of the Rachmaninoff Concerto No. 2 with the Philadelphia Orchestra," said Sellers, who lives in Los Angeles. "That was the first record I ever bought.

"Kapell has been in my consciousness all these years," he continued. "I was impressed with his orchestral style. His tone, especially as you hear it on records, was phenomenal. I suppose it was even more astonishing in the hall.

"I have that sound in my mind now. But when I came to establish this foundation, I wasn't thinking of Kapell. People told me it would be practical to name the foundation after a famous musician, and when I thought, I thought that Kapell symbolized what I admire in music."

Ironically, notes Sellers, the company that recorded Kapell, RCA, has no interest in reissuing any of his work. For this anniversary, the International Piano Archive, now at the

Richard Goode
Former Curtis Institute student

Gary Graffman
Internationally known pianist

University of Maryland, is issuing record made from tapes of a performance of a Carnegie Hall recital

After Kapell's death, Mann established annual memorial concerts feature young pianists at the Philadelphia Orchestra's summer ser and he endowed a chair in the ar Kapell's memory at Brandeis University. The Naumburg Foundation a competition named for Kape 1978, awarding the winning pi performances with several maj chestras.

NED ROREM

Dear Michael Sellers—

30 August 84

It's strange how intensely I recall the Kapell Memorial Concert of ten months ago. Strange, because although many of my friends played that evening I remember their living presence less vividly than the presence of William Kapell himself. He was evoked like a genie, which must have been the purpose of the concert.

What was evoked, of course, was the sight and sound of Willy I heard him play often in the 1940s; even now as I write I can still hear his <u>way</u> with a keyboard: that purposeful, shining, pliable strength, like Damascus steel, yet gentle as a child— a <u>good</u> child. I knew him personally—not well—through Eugene Istomin. (Though what does "to know well" mean? Willy seemed so dynamically alert that an hour with him was like a day with anyone else.) What I retain is the power, the almost-sexuality, of his attention. I once played some songs for him, somewhat intimidated but urged on by Eugene. After one hearing he knew them, words and music, better than I did, plying me with questions, not letting me off the hook. He cared.

Like most composers my interest in any performer lies ulti- mately in ~~their~~ his interest in new music. Willy was the first— and, alas, the only—big-time American pianist for whom, repertorially, the present was on a par with the past. These notions had receded with the decades until last fall's concert so successfully choreographed by you. William Kapell was our most important pianist. Thankyou for bringing him back.

If asked to provide something for publication, this is all I'd be able to say. You're welcome to it.

Warmly

Ned Rorem

The Kapell memorial attracted a distinguished audience. Critics came from as far away as Philadelphia, and several important composers, among them Ned Rorem, were in attendance. And there were pianists everywhere.

David Kapell, Fredric Mann and Rebecca Kapell Leigh immediately after the Symphony Space tribute.

(Above) At the 1986 opening of the Kapell collection, IPAM. Left to Right, back row: Mrs. Eugene Ormandy, Rebecca Leigh, Eugene Istomin, Dr. Anna Lou Dehavenon, Mrs. Fredric R. Mann, Bernard Kapell, David Kapell. Front row: Joshua Kapell, Matthew Kapell.

(Above) Anna Lou trekking in the Nepalese Himalayas in the 1990s. (Below) The Kapell grandchildren 1990: (foreground) David Alexander Leigh; (back row) Matthew Kapell, Elliot Leigh, Caitlin Kapell and Joshua Kapell. Note the resemblance between Matthew Kapell and his grandfather at a similiar age on page eight.

Copyright © 1947 (Renewed 1975) by Irving Penn.

Discography

By Allan Evans

A User's Guide: Traditional discographies list commercial recordings followed by performances from other sources. For William Kapell's legacy I have combined both; not only is it immaterial to whom the recording microphone belonged, for it is Kapell's art that is paramount, but by grouping all performances of a single work together one approaches a view of the frequency with which he played them. Asterisks preceding a date indicate a recording published by RCA/BMG or other specified labels. Performances listed by date alone are unpublished concert or home recordings. Unpublished RCA material is preceded by its matrix number ("mtx:"). Inclusion of take numbers preceded by a dash ("-2") indicate an accepted take other than the first. One television program with Kapell is available for viewing at the Museum of Broadcasting, New York as well as at the International Piano Archives at Maryland. The musical selections from this telecast have been incorporated into the discography.

An enigma: Jon M. Samuels of BMG observes that as RCA recording sessions after 1948 were made on tape, take numbers may be composites drawn from an earlier generation of session tapes. RCA logs reveal one or two takes yet do not document the original master tapes of entire sessions, which might include other takes, spoken words between artist and producer, even works not listed. As there are half a million tapes (master, takes, dubs, etc.) in BMG's archives, many unlabelled or unnumbered, it will be the task of future tape archaeologists (a sizeable team to say the least) to codify this awesome collection. This is a cause for great concern, as this invaluable legacy can easily fall victim to future corporate "cost-cutting" in which the expensive upkeep might suddenly be deemed a lesser priority.

My gratitude to Dr. Anna Lou Dehavenon and her family; Tim Page; John Pfeiffer; Neil Ratliff and the staff of the International Piano Archives at the University of Maryland; Donald Manildi; JoAnne Barry, archivist of the Philadelphia Orchestra; Bridget Carr, archivist of the Boston Symphony; Anibal Ramirez of the Museo Pablo Casals, San Juan, Puerto Rico; the New York Philharmonic Archives; Joe Salerno; Dr. Karl Miller; Jon M. Samuels; David Soyer; Seth Winner and Richard "Russ" Hornbeck for their invaluable assistance.

Albeniz:

Iberia: Evocacion.
*April 27, 1945. mtx: D5-RC-294. 78: DM 1101 (11-8866-B), HMV DB 21268/9. 45: WDM-1101. LP: LM-2588.

Triana.
Oct. 28, 1941. (incomplete). Unpublished.

Bach:

Concerto for 4 Claviers in A minor, BWV 1065.
May 20, 1950. Eugene List, Joseph Battista, Rosalyn Tureck, pianos. Milton Katims/NBC Strings. Unpublished.

Partita No. 2 in C minor, BWV 826.
Feb. 28, 1945. Unpublished.

Partita No. 4 in D, BWV 828. (Gigue omitted).
*Dec. 18, 1952, Mar. 10–12, 1953. mtx: E2-RC-1838/44. 45: ERA-199. LP: LM-1791 (part one of Gigue was recorded and remains unpublished).
1951. Buenos Aires. Allemande, Courante only. Unpublished.

Partita (unidentified): *Allemande.*
Dec. 20, 1951. mtx: E1-RB-4929, 7037/8. Unpublished.

Prelude & Fugue in C# minor
(Well Tempered Clavier Book I).
1940. Unpublished.
Oct. 28, 1941. Fugue excerpt. Unpublished.

Suite in A minor BWV 818.
Oct. 28, 1941. Fragment. Unpublished.
Feb. 28, 1945. Unpublished.
Jan. 7, 1947. D7-RC-7107-1 (Allemande), 7107-2 (Courante), 7108-1 (Sarabande simple), 7108-1A (Sarabande double), 7108-2 (Gigue). Unpublished.
*Mar. 21, 1947. LP: IPAM 1101.

Bach/Busoni:

Nun komm der Heiden Heiland
(Come, Thou Savior of Mankind)
Oct. 17, 1951. Unpublished.

Wachet Auf (Sleepers Awake)
Oct. 28, 1941. Unpublished.

Beethoven:

Concerto No. 2 in B♭, op. 19.
Jun. 23, 1946. Vladimir Golschmann/NBC Symphony. Unpublished.
*Jun. 24, 1946. Vladimir Golschmann/NBC Symphony. mtx: D6-RC-6004/5/6 (2)/7 (2)/8/9/10. Tk.2 on 6006/7. 78: DM-1132. 45: WDM-1132. LP: LM-12, LM-9026, VIC-1520.
Undated. Donald Voorhees/CBC Orch. Unpublished.

Concerto No. 3 in C minor, op. 37.
Apr. 26, 1937. Leon Barzin/National Orch. Assoc. 2nd & 3rd mvts. Unpublished.

Diabelli Variations, op. 120.
1940. Excerpts: Theme and Variation 3. Unpublished.
1949. Excerpts: Theme and Variation 1. Unpublished.

Sonata in D, op. 12 no. 1 for Violin and Piano.
*Jun. 20, 1953. Arthur Grumiaux, violin.
LP: DISCOCORP RR-547. CD: MUSIC & ARTS CD-689-4.

Variations (32) in C minor, WoO 80.
1940. Excerpts: Variations 24–32. Unpublished.

Variations (6) on an Original Theme in F, op. 34.
Undated home recording. Unpublished.

Brahms:

Piano Concerto no. 1 in D minor, op. 15.
Dec. 11, 1945. Eugene Ormandy/Philadelphia Orchestra. Unpublished.
*Apr. 12, 1953. Dimitri Mitropoulos/New York Philharmonic. LP: MJA 1966-3. CD: MELODRAM 18009, ARKADIA 736.

Intermezzo in A♭, op. 76 no. 3
*Mar. 21, 1947. LP: IPAM 1101.

Intermezzo in E, op. 116 no. 4.
*Mar. 21, 1947. LP: IPAM 1106. [Abbreviated]

Intermezzo in E, op. 116 no. 6.
*Apr. 27, 1945. mtx: D5-RC-293. 78: 11-9621-B.

Sonata No. 3 in F minor, op. 5.
Feb. 28, 1945. 2nd mvt. (last 12 bars missing). Unpublished.

Sonata in F minor, op. 120 No. 1 for Viola and Piano.
William Primrose, viola.
*May 7, 1946. mtx: D6-RC-5837/9, 40-2, 41-2, 42-2. 78: 11-9487/9. 78: DM-1106. LP: SMITHSONIAN LGR-9265.

Sonata in D minor, op. 108 for Violin and Piano.
Jascha Heifetz, violin.
*Nov. 29–30, 1950. mtx: EO-RC-0467-72.

78: DM-1523. 45: WDM-1523. LP: LM-71, LM-2836, ARM4-0947.

Chasins:

By the Brook.
Jun. 24, 1952. mtx: E2-RC-0222. Unpublished.

Dancing Bagpipes.
Jun. 24, 1952. mtx: E2-RC-0223. Unpublished.

Tricky Trumpet.
Jun. 24, 1952. mtx: E2-RC-0224. Unpublished.
Undated AFRS disc. Unpublished.

Waltz of the Rainbow.
Jun. 24, 1952. mtx: E2-RC-0221. Unpublished.

Chopin:

Barcarolle.
1940. Incomplete (measures 78 to end missing). Unpublished.

Mazurka no. 2 in C♯ minor, op. 6 no. 2.
Oct. 17, 1951. Unpublished.
*Dec. 20, 1951. mtx: E1-RB-4921. LP: LM-1865. CD: BMG 5998-2-RC.
Feb. 26, 1952. mtx: E1-RB-4921-2. Unpublished.

Mazurka no. 5 in B♭, op. 7 no. 1
1940. Unpublished.

Mazurka no. 6 in A minor, op. 7 no. 2.
Dec. 27, 1951. mtx: E1-RB-4922. Unpublished.
*Feb. 26, 1952. mtx: E1-RB-4922-2. 45: ERA-232. LP: LM-1865. CD: BMG 5998-2-RC.

Mazurka no. 9 in C, op. 7 no. 5
*Dec. 20, 1951. mtx: E1-RB-4921.
45: WDM-1715, ERA-105.
LP: LM-1715, IPAM 1108.
CD: BMG 5998-2-RC.

Mazurka no. 11 in E minor, op. 17 no. 2.
*Dec. 20, 1951. mtx: E1-RB-4920. LP: LM-1865. CD: BMG 5998-2-RC.

Mazurka no. 12 in A♭, op. 17 no. 3.
Dec. 27, 1951. mtx: E1-RB-4926. Unpublished.
*Feb. 26, 1952. mtx: E1-RB-4926-2.
LP: LM-1865. CD: BMG 5998-2-RC.

Mazurka no. 14 in G minor, op. 24 no. 1
*Dec. 20, 1951. mtx: E1-RB-4920.
45: WDM-1715. LP: LM-1715, IPAM 1108.

Mazurka no. 16 in A♭, op. 24, no. 3.
*Jun. 24, 1952. mtx: E2-RC-0219.
45: ERA-232. LP: IPAM 1108.

Mazurka no. 20 in D♭, op. 30, no. 3.
*Dec. 27, 1951. mtx: E1-RB-4925. LP: LM-1865. CD: BMG 5998-2-RC.

Mazurka no. 22 in G♯, minor op. 33 no. 1
*Jun. 24, 1952. mtx: E2-RC-0218. LP: LM-1865. CD: BMG 5998-2-RC.

Mazurka no. 24 in C, op. 33 no. 3
*Dec. 20, 1951. mtx: E1-RB-4919. 45: WDM-1715.
LP: LM-1715, IPAM 1108.

Mazurka no. 25 in B minor, op. 33 no. 4.
*Feb. 20, 1952. mtx: E1-RB-0159. 45: WDM-1715.
LP: LM-1715, IPAM 1108.

Mazurkas nos. 26 in C♯ minor and 27 in E minor, op. 41 nos. 1, 2.
*Feb. 20, 1952. mtx: E1-RB-0158. 45: ERA-213, French HMV A 95224. LP: LM-1865. CD: BMG 5998-2-RC.

Mazurka no. 31 in A♭, op. 50 no. 2
*Dec. 27, 1951. mtx: E1-RB-4924. LP: LM-1865. CD: BMG 5998-2-RC.

Mazurka no. 32 in C♯ minor, op. 50 no. 3
*Feb. 26, 1952. mtx: E1-RB-0162. 45: ERA-232. LP: LM-1865. CD: BMG 5998-2-RC.

Mazurka no. 35 in C minor, op. 56 no. 3.
*Dec. 27, 1951. mtx: E1-RB-4927. 45: WDM-1715, ERA-105. LP: LM-1715, IPAM 1108.

Mazurkas nos. 36 in A minor and 37 in A♭, op. 59 nos. 1, 2.
*Feb. 26, 1952. mtx: E1-RB-0163. 45: ERA-213, French HMV A 95224. LP: LM-1865, IPAM 1108.

Mazurka no. 40 in F minor, op. 63 no. 2
*Mar. 21, 1947. LP: IPAM 1106.
*Feb. 20, 1952. mtx: E1-RB-0160. LP: LM-1865, IPAM 1108.

Mazurka no. 41 in C♯ minor, op. 63 no. 3
*Feb. 26, 1952. mtx: E1-RB-0162. 45: ERA-232. LP: LM-1865, IPAM 1108.

Mazurka no. 43 in G minor, op. 67 no. 2.
*Jun. 24, 1952. mtx: E2-RC-0216. LP: LM-1865, IPAM 1108.

Mazurka no. 44 in C, op. 67 no. 3.
Dec. 27, 1951. mtx: E1-RB-4925. Unpublished.
*Feb. 20, 1952. mtx: E1-RB-4925-2.
45: WDM-1715. LP: LM-1715, IPAM 1108.

Mazurka no. 45 in A minor, op. 67 no. 4.
*Jun. 23, 1952. mtx: E2-RC-0213.

45: WDM-1715, ERA-105.
LP: LM-1715, IPAM 1108.

Mazurka no. 47 in A minor, op. 68 no. 2
*Feb. 20, 1952. mtx: E1-RB-0161. 45: ERA-232.
LP: LM-1865, IPAM 1108.

Mazurkas nos. 48 in F and 49 in F minor, op. 68 nos. 3, 4.
*Feb. 20, 1952. mtx: E1-RB-0160. 45: WDM-1715, ERA-105. LP: LM-1715, IPAM 1108.

Mazurka no. 50 in A minor, op. post.
*Dec. 27, 1951. mtx: E1-RB-4928. 45: WDM-1715, ERA-105.
*Feb. 20, 1952. mtx: E1-RB-4928-2. LP: LM-1865, IPAM 1108.

Mazurka no. 52 in B♭, op. post.
*Dec. 27, 1951. mtx: E1-RB-4923. LP: LM-1715, IPAM 1108.

Nocturne in B♭ minor, op. 9 no. 1.
*Feb. 28, 1945. LP: IPAM 1101.

Nocturne in E♭, op. 55 no. 2.
*Mar. 15, 1953. LP: MJA 1966-3.
Video (from Kinescope) Unpublished.
Undated. From an untraced RCA session. Unpublished.

Nocturne in B, op. 62 no. 1.
1940. Unpublished. (Last 14 measures missing.)

Nocturne in E, op. 62 no. 2.
Mar. 21, 1947. Unpublished.

Polonaise in A♭, Op. 53
1940. Unpublished

Sonata No. 2 in B♭, minor, op. 35.
*Oct. 22, 1953. CD: BMG 5998-2-RC.

Sonata No. 3 in B minor, op. 58.
Mar. 21, 1947. (Excerpts). Unpublished.
Jun. 14, 1949. Unpublished.
*Sep. 22, 1953. LP: OPUS MLG-83.

First movement:
Dec. 21, 1949. mtx: D9-RC-2121 (part one). Unpublished.
*May 19, 1951. mtx: E1-RC-3706/7-3. 45: WDM-1715. CD: BMG 5998-2-RC.

Second movement:
Dec. 21, 1949. mtx: D9-RC-2119/20. Unpublished.
*May 21, 1951. mtx: E1-RC-3708. CD: BMG 5998-2-RC.

Third movement:
May 21, 1951. mtx: E1-RC-3709/10. Unpublished.

Jul. 5, 1951. mtx: E1-RC-3709-2,3. 3710-2,3,4. Unpublished.
*Jun. 23, 1952. mtx: E2-RC-0211 (part one). 45: WDM 1715. CD: BMG 5998-2-RC.
Jun. 24, 1952. mtx: E2-RC-0280 (part two). Unpublished.

Fourth movement:
Jun. 14, 1948. Unpublished.
*Jun. 4, 1951. mtx: E1-RB-3711. 45: WDM-1715. CD: BMG 5998-2-RC.

Valse in E♭, op. 18.
Jun. 24, 1952. mtx: E2-RC-0220. Unpublished.

Debussy:

Children's Corner Suite.
1951, Buenos Aires. Unpublished.

Dr. Gradus ad Parnassum.
May 19, 1951. mtx: E1-RB-4458 (or E1-RB-2169). Unpublished.

Jimbo's Lullaby.
*Dec. 21, 1950. mtx: EO-RC-1967. 78: 12-3212-A. 45: 49-3212-A.
Jun. 4, 1951. mtx: E1-RB-2187. Unpublished.
Jul. 5, 1951. mtx: E1-RB-2187-2. Unpublished.
Dec. 20, 1951. mtx: E1-RB-4653. Unpublished.

The Snow is Dancing.
May 19, 1951. mtx: E1-RB-2171. Unpublished.
Jun. 4, 1951. mtx: E1-RB-2171-2. Unpublished.
Dec. 20, 1951. mtx: E1-RB-4655. Unpublished.

Serenade to the Doll.
Dec. 18, 1950. mtx: EO-RC-1966. Unpublished.
May 19, 1951. mtx: E1-RB-4459. Unpublished.
Jun. 4, 1951. mtx: E1-RB-2170-2. Unpublished.
Jul. 5, 1951. mtx: E1-RB-2170-3. Unpublished.
Dec. 20, 1951. mtx: E1-RB-4654. Unpublished.

The Little Shepherd.
*Dec. 20, 1950. mtx: EO-RC-1968. 78: 12-3212B. 45: 49-3212-B.
Jun. 4, 1951. mtx: E1-RB-2189. Unpublished.
Jul. 5, 1951. mtx: E1-RB-2189-2. Unpublished.
Dec. 20, 1951. mtx: E1-RB-4656. Unpublished.

Golliwogg's Cake-Walk.
*Dec. 20, 1950. mtx: EO-RC-1968.
78: 12-3212-B.
45: 49-3212-B.
Jun. 4, 1951. mtx: E1-RB-2188. Unpublished.

Estampes: Soirée dans Grenade.
*Feb. 28, 1945. LP: IPAM 1101.

Suite Bergamasque.
Oct. 17, 1951. Unpublished.

Falla:

Four Spanish Pieces: Aragonesa, Cubana.
1951, Buenos Aires. Unpublished.

Nights in the Gardens of Spain.
*Nov. 13, 1949. Leopold Stokowski/New York Phil. LP: OPUS MLG-71, SMITHSONIAN NYP 821/2.

Three-Cornered Hat:

Farrucca.
1951 Buenos Aires. Unpublished.

Miller's Dance.
Oct. 17, 1951. Unpublished.

Granados:

Goyescas: The Maiden and the Nightingale.
Mar. 21, 1947. Unpublished.
Oct. 17, 1951. Unpublished.

Khachaturian:

Piano Concerto.
Oct. 29, 1943. Serge Koussevitsky/Boston S.O. Unpublished.
Jan. 1, 1945. Serge Koussevitsky/Boston S.O. mtx: D5-RC-600 (2), 601 (2), 602 (2), 603 (2), 604, 605, 606 (2), 607. Unpublished.
May 20, 1945. Frank Black/NBC S.O. Unpublished.
*Apr. 19, 1946. Serge Koussevitsky/Boston S.O. mtx: D6-RC-5700/1/2 (2)/3 (2)/4/5/6/7. (Tk.2 on 5702/3.)
78: Set 1084. 45: WDM 1084. LP: LM-1006, LM-2588, AGM1-5266. CD: BMG 9026-60921-2.
Nov. 24, 1946. Artur Rodzinski/New York Philharmonic. Unpublished.

Liszt:

Hungarian Rhapsody no. 6 in D♭.
Oct. 28, 1941. (Excerpt). Unpublished.
Oct. 27, 1942. Unpublished.

Hungarian Rhapsody no. 11 in A minor.
*May 19, 1951. mtx: E1-RC-3712. 45: ERA-199. LP: LM-1791, LM-2585.
Jul. 5, 1951. mtx: E1-RC-3712-2. (part one) Unpublished.
1951, Buenos Aires. Unpublished.

Mephisto Waltz no. 1.
*March 19, 1945. mtx: D5-RC-191, 192 (2), 193. Tks. 1,2,1. (?) 78: 11-9456, 9457-A. 78: DM-1101, HMV DB 21268/9. 45: 49-1190/91. LP: LM-1058, LM-1791, LM-2588. CD: BMG 9026-60921-2.

Sonnetto del Petrarca 104 in E.
*Aug. 22, 1947. mtx: D7-RC-7820/1. 78: 12-0342. 45: 49-0384.

Mendelssohn:

Song Without Words, op. 62 no. 6 "Spring Song"
1940. Unpublished.

Song Without Words, op. 67 no. 5.
Dec. 18, 1950. mtx: EO-RC-1965. Unpublished.

Mozart:

Piano Concerto no. 12 in A, K.414: (2nd & 3rd mvts.)
*Apr. 23, 1950. Pierre Monteux/Los Angeles Phil. LP: IPA 507.

Piano Concerti (nos. 12, 17, 20, 27)
1940. Piano solo, excerpts. Unpublished.

Piano Quartet in E♭, K.493.
*Jun. 27, 1953. Arthur Grumiaux, violin; Milton Thomas, viola; Paul Tortelier, cello.
LP: DISCOCORP RR-547. CD: MUSIC & ARTS CD-689-4.

Sonata in C, K.330.
1940. 1st movement excerpt. Unpublished.
*Mar. 21, 1947. LP: IPAM 1101.
Oct. 17, 1951. Unpublished.

Sonata in B♭, K.570.
Undated. AFRS disc. Unpublished.
Mar. 12, 1953. mtx: E3-RC-2147/8. (2nd & 3rd mvts.) Unpublished.

Mussorgsky:

Pictures at an Exhibition.
Oct. 17, 1951. Unpublished (complete).
*Jul. 21, 1953. LP: OPUS MLG-83.
(Incomplete: ending taken from Horowitz disc.)

Napolitano:

El Gato.
Mar. 21, 1947. Unpublished.
Jun. 18, 1950. Unpublished.
Mar. 15, 1953. Unpublished. Video (from Kinescope): Unpublished.

Nin:

Danza Iberica.
Feb. 28, 1945. Unpublished.

Palmer:

Toccata Ostinato.
*Feb. 28, 1945. LP: IPAM 1101.

Prokofiev:

Concerto no. 3.
Feb. 22, 1947. Eugene Ormandy/Philadelphia Orch. Unpublished.
*Jan. 7, 1949. Antal Dorati/Dallas Symphony. mtx: D9-RC-908/13. 78: M-1326. 45: WDM-1326. LP: LM-1058, VIC 1520, AGM1-5266. CD: BMG 9026-60921-2.
Feb. 20, 1949. Leopold Stokowski/New York Phil. Unpublished.
Feb. 20, 1951. William Strickland/Nashville Symph. (Incomplete) Unpublished.
Mar. 20–21, 1953. Richard Burgin/Boston Symph. Orch. Unpublished.

Sonata No. 7, op. 83: Excerpts from first two movements.
*Mar. 21, 1947. LP: IPAM 1106.

Rachmaninoff:

Concerto no. 2 in C minor.
Oct. 8, 1944. Jay Blackton/RCA Orch. 1st mvt. Unpublished.
Mar. 25, 1945. Leon Barzin/National Orch. Assoc. Unpublished.
Jun. 14, 1948. Donald Voorhees/Bell Telephone Orch. 1st mvt. Unpublished.
Jun. 18, 1950. Alfred Wallenstein/NBC Symph. 1st mvt. Unpublished.
*Jul. 7, 1950. William Steinberg/Robin Hood Dell Orch. mtx: EO-RC-1223/32. 78: DM-1418. 45: WDM-1418. LP: LMX-1097.
Feb. 4, 1951. John Barnett/Los Angeles Phil. 1st mvt. Unpublished.
Feb. 25, 1951. Leonard Bernstein/New York Phil. Unpublished.

Concerto no. 3 in D minor.
*Apr. 13, 1948. Sir Ernest MacMillan/Toronto Symph. Orch. LP: IPA 507.
Sep. 30 or Oct. 1, 1953. Bernard Heinze/Victorian (Melbourne) Symph. Orch. Unpublished.
1953. Unidentified conductor/unspecified Australian Orchestra. Unpublished. (Cadenza and missing fragments.)

Prelude in C# minor, op. 3 no. 2.
*Dec. 11, 1944. mtx: D4-RC-544-4. 78: 11-8824-A.
*Mar. 19, 1945. mtx: D4-RC-544-5. 78: 11-8824-A. 45: 49-1190-B, 49-0264-A.

Rhapsody on a Theme of Paganini.
Oct. 28, 1944. Eugene Ormandy/Philadelphia Orch. Unpublished.
Oct. 28, 1945. Artur Rodzinski/New York Phil. Unpublished.
*Jun. 27, 1951. Fritz Reiner/Robin Hood Dell Orch. mtx: E1-RC-3789 (2)/90/91/92 (2)/93/94 (2). 78: DM-1576. 45: WDM 1576. LP: LM-126, LM-9026. LM-2588 (18th Var. only.)

Sonata for Cello and Piano in G minor, op. 19.
Edmund Kurtz, cello.
*Apr. 23–24, 1947. mtx: D7-RC-7455, 56-2, 57-1 & 2, 58, 59-2, 60-2, 61/2. 78: M-1261. 45: WDM-1261. LP: LM-1074.

Scarlatti:

Sonata (unidentified)
Dec. 21, 1949. mtx: D9-RC-2123. Unpublished.

Sonata L.23.
1940. Unpublished.
Mar. 15, 1953. Unpublished. Video (from Kinescope): Unpublished.

Schubert:

Impromptu in A♭, op. 142 no. 2.
*Dec. 18, 1952, Mar. 10–12, 1953. mtx: E2-RC-2235. 45: ERA-199. LP: LM-1791.

Ländler op. 171, nos. 1–7, 9.
*Jul. 3, 1952. mtx: E2-RC-0226/34. LP: ERA-199, LM 1791.

Lieder (unspecified).
Jun. 16, 1953. Maria Stader. Unpublished. (Prades Festival).

Moment musical (unidentified).
Dec. 21, 1949. mtx: D9-RC-2818. Unpublished.

Schumann:

Carnaval: Chopin.
1940. Unpublished.

Kinderszenen: Träumerei.
1940. Unpublished.
Jun. 18, 1950. Unpublished.

Quintet for Piano and Strings in E♭, op. 44.
Nov. 11, 1951. Fine Arts Quartet. Unpublished.

Romance in F♯, op. 28 no. 2.
1940. Unpublished.
*Feb. 28, 1945. LP: IPAM 1106.
April 27, 1945. mtx: D5-RC-292 (2). Unpublished.
Jan. 7, 1947. mtx: D7-RC-7109 (2). Unpublished.
Dec. 21, 1949. mtx: D9-RC-2118. Unpublished.

Shostakovitch:

Piano Concerto no. 1, op. 35.
*Dec. 1, 1945. Eugene Ormandy/Philadelphia Orchestra. LP: OPUS MLG-71.

Three Preludes from op. 54: nos. 5, 10, 24.
*Dec. 11, 1944. mtx: D4-RC-545-5. 78: 11-8824-B. 45: 49-0254.
*Feb. 28, 1945. LP: IPAM 1101.
Mar. 19, 1945. mtx: D5-RC-190-1. Unpublished.
*Undated. LP: MJA 1966-3.

Strauss:

Burlesque (through measure 549).
Feb. 1, 1948. Fritz Reiner/Pittsburgh Symph. Orch. Unpublished.

Troyani:

Milonga.
1951 Buenos Aires. Unpublished.

INTERVIEWS:

Aug. 10, 1944. Kapell speaks before performing Rachmaninoff's Second Concerto.
1952 or 1953. Kapell as guest on a New York radio program. (30' 10").

MISCELLANY:

One minute of Kapell playing Boogie-Woogie exists on an acetate disc.

APPENDIX:

Performances which may exist.

Beethoven:

Concerto No. 2 in B♭, op. 19.
Nov. 10/11, 1949. Leopold Stokowski/New York Philharmonic.

Khachaturian:

Piano Concerto.
Apr. 8, 1944. Eugene Ormandy/Philadelphia Orch.

Mozart:

Concerto no. 17 in G, K.453.
Nov. 27/28, 1952. Dimitri Mitropoulos/New York Philharmonic.
June 30, 1953. Pablo Casals/Prades Festival Orch.

Prokofiev:

Concerto no. 3.
Feb. 15/16, 1951. Leonard Bernstein/New York Philharmonic.

Rachmaninoff:

Concerto no. 2.
Mar. 23/24, 1944. Artur Rodzinski/New York Philharmonic.
Jun. 18, 1944. Fritz Reiner/New York Philharmonic.
Feb. 17/18, 1949. Leopold Stokowski/New York Philharmonic.

Tchaikovsky:

Concerto no. 1.
Nov. 22, 1946. Artur Rodzinski/New York Philharmonic.
Nov. 16, 1949. Eugene Ormandy/Philadelphia Orchestra.

AFTERWORD:

A tape made from acetates of Kapell's debut recital is rumored to exist. Since fragments of Toscanini's concerts with the Palestine Symphony are extant, Israeli archives and collections may contain material from Kapell's 1953 tour. I hope this discography will help other surviving Kapell recordings to emerge and be published.

Discography © 1992 by Allan Evans

INDEX

Academy of Music, 5
Albeniz, Isaac, 5
American music, 113
Archives. *See* International Piano Archives at Maryland (IPAM)
Argus-Courier, 169
Australia, 30, 114: final tour, 160; recital notes, 157; tour, 52-57; tour programs, 154-155; tour reviews, 161; zoo, 56-57
Australian Women's Weekly, 70

Bach, Johann Sebastian, 5: D major Partita, 113; Partita No. 4, 114; Suite in A Minor, 5; "Well Tempered Clavier," 5
Ballade in F Major (Chopin), 6
BBC eulogy, 163-164
Beethoven, Ludwig van: Piano Concerto No. 2, 28, 30; violin sonatas, 114
Bendiner, Alfred, 117
Berger, Arthur, 133
Berkshires, 38, 45
Bernstein, Leonard, 27, 79, 85, 181
Biancolli, Louis, 170
Birth, 3
Bohm, Jerome D., 6, 24
Boston Symphony Orchestra, 28
Brahms, Johannes, 5: D Minor Sonata (Op.108), 126; F Minor Sonata for Piano and Viola, 30; Sonata in C (Op.1), 5; violin sonatas, 114, 126
British Commonwealth Pacific Airline DC-6, 115
Brooklyn, 9
Buenos Aires, 103-104, 105
Byronic side of Kapell, 37

Cadman, Charles Wakefield, 49
California, 12, 27
Canton Island, 115
Carnegie Hall, 5, 43: concert, 29; program, 42

Caruso, Enrico: "Over There" recording, 30
Casa de Mañana, 4
Casals, Pablo, 28, 114, 153
Cassidy, Claudia, 29, 171
Central Park, 8
Chasins, Abram, 33
Chicago, 97: Symphony, 30; University of, 30
Chicago Tribune, 29
Children's Corner (Debussy), 113
Chopin, Frederic, 5: B-flat Minor Sonata, 28; B Minor Sonata (Op.58), 113; F Major Ballade, 6; "Funeral March" Sonata in B-flat (Op.35), 115; Mazurkas, 113; Nocturne in B-flat Minor, 14
Classical music commercialization, 30
Clavier, 4
Cleveland, 83
Cliburn, Van, 180
Columbia Artists, 27: promotional flyers, 58-59
Columbia Concerts, 27, 34
Columbia Grammar School, 4, 11
Compositions: early, 13; "Song Without Words," 18-19
Concertos, piano: first recording, 28; K.414 (Mozart), 114; Khachaturian, 27-28, 36; Prokofiev, 79; Rachmaninoff, 30; Second Piano (Beethoven), 28;
Concerts: Latin America, 118-119; outdoor, 85. *See also* Australia; Buenos Aires; Tours
Connecticut, 47
Contract, 34, 131
Cooke, Alistair, 163
Copland, Aaron: eulogy to Kapell, 173; Letter, 45; Piano Fantasy, 45, 113, 164, 176; Piano Sonata, 113; Piano Variations, 45, 113; Sonata, 45, 113; Variations, 113
Czerny, Carl, 112

Dallas Symphony Orchestra, 144
Death, 163-165, 166-171

Debussy, Claude: Children's Corner, 113
Dedication (Copland Piano Fantasy), 45
Dehavenon, Anna Lou, 1, 4, 5, 28, 29, 187. *See also* Kapell, Anna Lou; Melson, Rebecca Anna Lou
Dello Joio, Norman, 113
Denver, 83
DePaul University, 30
Depression (The), 3
Diaries: later, 27; publication of excerpts, 164; response to reviews, 29
Discography, 189-195. *See also* Recordings
Downes, Olin, 5, 85
Dubman, Laura. *See* Fratti, Laura

Effinger, Cecil, 83
Etude Magazine, 120-121
Europe, 52, 94

Family life, 129, 150-151
Farrell, Richard, 55
Fiji, 115
Fleisher, Leon, 28
Florida, 151, 163
France, 29, 114
France Musique, 164
Fratti, Laura, 44, 112, 114
Freeport, Illinois, 29
Fried, Alexander, 169
"Funeral March" (Chopin), 115

Gardiner, Eunice, 115, 161
Gerber, Leslie, 164
Golschmann, Vladimir, 30
Goode, Richard, 182
Gossip columnists, 30
Gould, Glenn, 5, 114
Gould, Morton, 46
Graffman, Gary, 30, 182
Greiner, Alexander (Sascha), 123, 163
Gromyko, Andrei, 28
Grumiaux, Arthur, 114
Gutierrez, Horacio, 30, 97

Health, 152
Heifetz, Jascha, 114, 126
Hendl, Walter, 144
Herbert, Victor, 30
Hermann, Claude, 164
Hess, Myra, 138-139
Honolulu, 115
Hope, Constance, 30, 62, 163
Horowitz, Vladimir, 28, 30, 97, 111-112, 114, 125
Hume, Paul, 169

"In Search of a Lost Pianist" (Kaminski), 165
Insecurities, 111
International Piano Archives at Maryland (IPAM), 1, 30, 186: Kapell archives, 164
International William Kapell Piano Competition, 164

Interviews, 164-165
IPAM. See[i] International Piano Archives at Maryland (IPAM)
Israel, 29, 114, 150
Istomin, Eugene, 28, 114, 163, 174, 181, 186
Iturbi, Jose, 3
Ives, Charles Edward, 113

Joseffy, Rafael, 30
Judson, Arthur, 34, 131: contract with, 27
Judson Agency, 163
Juilliard School, 4, 5, 14, 34, 38, 112, 145, 164

Kaminski, Piotr, 164
Kapell (William) Foundation for Contemporary Music and Musicians, 164
Kapell, Anna Lou, 104, 111, 114, 130, 158-159, 163, 164, 180, 186: letter of consolation to, 172. *See also* Dehavenon, Anna Lou; Melson, Rebecca Anna Lou
Kapell, Bernard, 3, 4, 8, 29, 163, 186
Kapell, Caitlin, 187
Kapell, David, 108, 158, 186, 186
Kapell, Edith Wolfson (Mouletski), 3, 8, 11, 151
Kapell, Hyman (Harry), 3, 9, 151
Kapell, Joshua, 186, 187
Kapell, Matthew, 186, 187
Kapell, Rebecca Ellen, 111, 186
Kapell archives. *See* International Piano Archives at Maryland (IPAM)
Kapell bookstore, 13
Kapell collection, 186
Kapell family, 186
Kapell-Leigh, Rebecca, 186
Kastendieck, Miles, 133
Khachaturian, Aram, 49: first recording of Piano Concerto, 28; Piano Concerto, 27-28, 36
Koussevitzky, Serge, 28
Kurtz, Efrem, 27
Kuyper, George, 30-31
Kuyper, Mildred, 30-31

LaFollette, Dorothy Anderson, 3, 4, 5, 12, 41
La Jolla, 4, 12, 108
Latin America concerts, 118-119
Lawsuit, 164, 178-179
Leigh, David Alexander, 187
Leigh, Elliot, 187
Leland, Phillip, 145
Lessons, first, 3
Letter From America (Cooke), 163
Lewis, Jessie, 30
Lewisohn Stadium, 27, 79
Lhevinne, Josef, 4
Lhevinne, Rosina, 4
Liszt, Franz: "Mephisto Waltz No. 1," 28; Eleventh Rhapsody, 113
Loesser, Arthur, 82-83
Log, tour pianos, 125
London Symphony Orchestra, 106

Long Island, 8
Los Angeles, 145, 175
Lowenthal, Jerome, 4, 112, 145, 182
Lunde, Solveig (Dorothy; Dophey), 5, 14

"Madam" (See Samaroff, Olga)
Mann, Fredric, 29, 34, 112, 130, 163, 186
Marriage, 31, 96-99
Masselos, William, 113, 183
Mazurkas (Chopin), 113
Media, 91-93
Medtner, Nikolai Karlovich, 5
Melbourne, 114
Melson, Rebecca Anna Lou, 30, 31, 96-99. *See also* Dehavenon, Anna Lou; Kapell, Anna Lou
Memorial program, 180, 185
"Memories of William Kapell" (Lowenthal), 4
Mennin, Peter, 113
Mephisto Waltz No. 1 (Liszt), 28: reissue, 164
Meurice Hotel, 163
Mewton-Wood, Noel, 55
Miller, Gladys, 70
Monteux, Pierre, 122
Morin, Phillippe, 164
Mozart, Wolfgang Amadeus, 153: childhood response to, 3; Concerto (K.414), 114
Music To My Eyes (Bendiner), 117
Musical focus, 111
Musicale, informal, 22
Mussorgsky, Modeste Petrovich, 29
My Many Years (Rubinstein), 4

Naumberg, Walter W., 20
Naumburg (Walter W.) Foundation, 6: International Competition, 164, 180; Musical Award, 5, 21
NBC: Bell Telephone Hour, 101; Symphony, 90
New York, 27, 83: public schools, 11
New York Herald Tribune, 6, 24, 29, 133, 141
New York Philharmonic, 27, 27, 47
New York Sun, 24, 133
New York Times, 5, 25, 29, 115, 133, 164: recital review, 112-113
New Zealand, 55
Nocturne in B-flat Minor (Chopin), 14
Nosworthy, Emily, 11

O'Connell, Charles, 5
O'Neill, Ruth, 163
Omnibus, 164
Orchestra Hall, 30: recital, 86
Orkin, Ruth, rehearsal photographs, 78-81
Ormandy, Eugene, 5, 27, 40, 89, 186: letter to Anna Lou, 172
Orth, Peter, 164, 180
Other interests, 29

P.S. 6, 11
Paris, 44
Partitas (Bach): D Major, 113; No. 4, 114
Pennsylvania Station, 163

Perkins, Francis, 133
Persichetti, Vincent, 113
Pfeiffer, Jack, 114
Philadelphia: Conservatory, 4, 14; Orchestra, 5, 27, 40, 85; program, 36
Philipp, Isidor, 29
Piano Fantasy (Copland), 45, 113, 164, 176; Variations, 45, 113
Piano Quarterly, 164
Piatigorsky, Gregor, 114
Picasso, Pablo, 29, 130
Poem to "Madam," 16
Political views, 29
Portland, 97
Prades Festival, 114, 153, 174
Press books, 50-51
Primrose, William, 30
Prokofiev, Sergei, 30, 89: Piano, Concerto No.3, 79
Publicity, 30, 62-73, 135-137. *See also* Reviews

Queensland Symphony Orchestra, 156

Rachmaninoff, Sergei, 5, 89: Piano Concerto No. 2, 30; Rhapsody, 31
Radio broadcasts, 40, 91
RCA Victor, 5, 43, 60-61, 90, 114, 115
Recitals: final, 142-143; first, 4
Recordings, 164, 164-165, 178-179: Beethoven Piano Concerto No. 2, 30; Brahms F minor Sonata for Piano and Viola, 30; early, 43; Khachaturian Piano Concerto, 28; late, 109. *See also* Discography
Reed College, 30
Reiner, Fritz, 27, 47
Religion, 29
Report card, 10
Residence, 130, 148-149
Reviews: by musicians, 83-84; Town Hall debut, 24. *See also* Publicity
Rhapsodies: Eleventh (Liszt), 113; (Rachmaninoff), 31
Rhoads, Shirley, 114, 183
Rice, Joel, 145
Robin Hood Dell, 5
Rodzinski, Artur, 47
Rorem, Ned, 113, 185
Royal Albert Hall, 106
Rubinstein, Arthur, 4, 44, 114
Ruggles, Carl, 113

Samaroff, Olga, 4, 5, 14, 17, 27, 34: letters from, 74-75; letter to editor of *Times*, 29; memorial concert, 112, 128
San Francisco, 115, 163
San Francisco Examiner, 169
Sargent, Sir Malcolm, 55, 106
Saturday Review, 172
Schirmer (G.) Music Publishers, 13
Schnabel, Artur, 28
Scholarship endowment, 41
Schonberg, Harold C., 112, 132
Schuster, Joseph, 175

Scrapbooks, press, 30
Sellers, Michael, 164, 183
Serkin, Rudolf, 28, 111
Sessions, Roger, 113
Shostakovich, Dmitri, 5
Sinatra, Frank, 30, 70
Sjveda, Jim, 164
Smoking, 152
South America, 52; tour, 100, 104-105; tour program, 103.
    See also Australia; Buenos Aires; Tours
South Carolina, 35
St. Michel de Cuxa, 153
Stader, Maria, 114
Steinway, 28, 122, 125, 127, 163
Stevenson, Adlai, 29
Stokowski, Leopold, 27: collaboration, 61
Straus, Noel, 29
Student recital, Kapell's class, 145
Sydney, 114
Sydney Daily Telegraph, 115
Symphony Space, 164: memorial program, 180-182; tribute, 186

Tanglewood, 164
Tarnowsky, Sergei, 30, 97
Taubman, Howard, 5, 6, 25
Teaching, 112: techniques, 112
Teatro Colon, 102-103
"Technique and Musicianship" (Kapell), 120-121

Thompson, Oscar, 24
Thomson, Virgil, 29, 83, 87, 113, 140-141, 170
Time Magazine, 171
Tours: international, 52-57; schedule, 94-95. *See also*
    Australia; Buenos Aires; South America
Town Hall, 21, 112: debut, 5, 33; recital program, 23
Tri-County Concerts Association, 39
Tributes, 166-171

Uninsky, Alexander, 30, 97
United States/Soviet Union United Front, 28
University of Chicago, 30
Upper East Side, 8
USO concert, 35

Victor Talking Machine Company, 4. *See also* RCA
    Victor
Villa-lobos, Heitor, 49

Washington Post, 169
Well Tempered Clavier (Bach), 5
WKCR-FM, 164: Kapell festival, 1
WNYC-FM, interview broadcast, 1
World War II, 28, 35

Yale Universtiy, 113
Yorkville Settlement Music School, 3
Youth Contest, 5